TWO S

of

EVERYTHING

TWO STORIES
of
EVERYTHING

*The Competing Metanarratives
of Islam and Christianity*

DUANE ALEXANDER MILLER

credo
house publishers

Published in the United States by Credo House Publishers,
a division of Credo Communications LLC, Grand Rapids, Michigan
credohousepublishers.com

ISBN: 978-1-625860-96-5

Cover and interior design by Sharon VanLoozenoord

First edition

In spite of all the dishonour,

the broken standards, the broken lives,

The broken faith in one place or another,

There was something left that was more than the tales

Of old men on winter evenings.

—T. S. ELIOT

TABLE OF CONTENTS

PREFACE

Standing on the lawn in front of the church the man gripped my hand and looked me in the eye and said, "I am a Jew, and a Christian, and a Muslim."

This man had vigorously opposed me teaching on Islam at his church (which is also the church our family belongs to). This was new to me. I had been teaching on Islam and Christianity at churches for going on a decade at this point, and had never had anyone say this sort of thing to me! At the heart of his case against me was that it is un-Christian to critically examine the faith of another community.

During one Sunday school session when my wife was sharing about her experience as a woman living among Muslims in the Arab world he stood up and opposed her. During one of my lectures he did the same thing to me. This made everyone feel nervous and awkward. But it did affirm me in the conviction that a critical and new re-visioning of Islam and Christianity is both timely and helpful, and that while I am critical of both Islam and Christianity, I make a genuine attempt to be fair.

In any case, it was after this series of seven Sunday school sessions that I really started to think that I needed to set down this material in a more concrete form than just lectures. It was after that event that a decision to write a book was made.

But the genesis of the *ideas* outlined in this book goes back quite a bit further. I was teaching at Nazareth Evangelical Theological Seminary some years ago. We had a visiting group from Italy and I was presenting a lecture to them comparing the narratives and metanarratives of Islam and Christianity. My friend Scott Bridger asked if he could cite the material; I said that beyond an outline and a lecture I did not have anything written down. But there was enough interest that I dashed off a brief summary of the material and that was published with the somewhat bland title of 'Narrative and Metanarrative in Christianity and Islam' (*St Francis Magazine*, Vol 6:3, June 2010).

I believe this approach of "comparative metanarratives" is more fruitful than that of "comparative religions." And so, I will not treat themes topically— God, prophets, rituals, holy writings, etc. Rather, I will treat them chronologically, or better yet, narratively—as the story develops. Because these are stories of everything, they each propose that *your* own life is part of their metanarrative, and as such demand that you make a decision and take a stand regarding how you relate to them. I am a Christian, and my conviction that the Christian metanarrative is more convincing than that of Islam may be apparent from time to time. However, this book is *not* an attempt to establish the superiority of Christianity, nor it is a polemic against Islam. There is only one place in the book where I explicitly explain why I find the Christian metanarrative more compelling than that of Islam. A secondary theme is my conviction that the West, a civilization characterized by a secular humanist metanarrative, is irreversibly moribund.

But I digress. Subsequent to that brief article in *SFM* I published a number of articles on Anglicanism in the Middle East but my main focus was on researching, writing, and then (worst of all) editing my PhD. This was gradually accomplished under the able guidance of Dr. Elizabeth Koepping at New College in Edinburgh. The thesis was defended in September of 2013, modest corrections were made, the final version was submitted, and the degree was awarded in 2014. That thesis, titled *Living among the Breakage: Contextual Theology-making and ex-Muslim Christians*, was done, and I found myself with time for other writing projects.

In October of 2013 my family and I moved back to the USA after many years living overseas. This allowed us to attend our home church in San Antonio again, after a long absence. Christ Church, which is where I met the man who was "a Jew, a Christian, and a Muslim," asked me to present some teachings on Islam and Christianity and afforded me a generous seven Sunday school sessions to do this. This allowed me (or required me) to explore in greater depth the theme of the comparative metanarratives (rather than comparative religions).

Several people asked to buy my book on the topic and after some prayer and reflection I decided that the time had arrived to commit myself to a substantial expansion of that slim article from *St Francis Magazine*. Finally, the epigraph by Eliot is used with permission.[1]

Duane Alexander Miller
The Anglican Cathedral of the Redeemer, Madrid
Fifth Monday of Mozarabic Advent, 2017

---

1   Excerpt from "Choruses from 'The Rock'" from *Collected Poems 1909-1962* by T. S. Eliot. Copyright 1936 by Houghton Mifflin Harcourt Publishing Company. Copyright renewed 1964 by Thomas Stearns Eliot. Reprinted by permission of Houghton Mifflin Harcourt. All rights reserved.

INTRODUCTION

People often talk of Islam and Christianity as competing *religions*, and compare their *doctrines and practices*. When I moved to the Middle East ten years ago I shared this opinion. But over that time I have found this approach to be deficient. Which is not to say it is wrong, but it fails to grasp the genius of either of these collections of doctrines and practices. Is there a more nuanced, effective way to view the relationship between Christianity and Islam? What other option do we have? In this book I will outline the *stories* that Islam and Christianity tell. Furthermore, all of these stories (or narratives) find themselves included in a great story of everything, which is to say a metanarrative. Islam and Christianity, whatever they may be, certainly do propose to tell a grand story of everything, from the creation of the world and time all the way to the consummation of history and the eternal fate of human souls.

I believe that forcing Islam and Christianity into the Enlightenment category of "religion" is a harmful move. This is not to say that we can never use the word "religion" to speak of Islam and Christianity, which are commonly called religions. Rather, the Enlightenment influence on religion, which made religions *ipso facto* the sort of things that could be privatized and cut off from the public life, is misleading and inauthentic. The thinkers of the Enlightenment (early 1600s through late 1700s) claimed to emphasized analysis, reason, and individualism, and argued that the public sphere should operate according to reason and science, whereas the subjective opinions of faith (which can't be proved either way) should be kept to one's self or one's religious community, which is to say the private sphere.

This compartmentalization of faith and reason—treating them (incorrectly) as if they were two different sources of knowledge with little or no relation to each other—betrays the genius at the heart of both of these movements. They both, at their very core, (and those are very different cores, I will argue) resist privatization[1] and compartmentalization. The Enlightenment vision was that such a

---

1   That is, a person should keep one's religious views private, or to themselves. Neither Muhammad nor Jesus would ever countenance such a concept.

society would be able to move beyond the superstition of medieval Christendom into a brave new world of reason, analysis, individualism, and modernity. In two words, the world of *secular humanism*. Secular because the governance of society comes from this world (*saecula* in Latin), and *humanist* because the human individual is the center of each person's universe, rather than God, or the Kingdom of God, or his Law/Torah/Shari'a. This project of discerning the "objective reason" from the "subjective religious faith" is, from the very beginning, an impossible task. This is the case because the very criteria used to differentiate faith from reason are always and already culturally situated. Secular humanism is, in other words, just another myth, but a powerful one. In the words of the great prophet and bishop Lesslie Newbigin:

> The secular society is a myth, and it has the power of a myth to blind people to realities. A powerful myth, such as this, has in it the power [of] "principalities and powers." Christian affirmation in this context requires the unmasking of the powers. It calls for a new kind of enlightenment, namely the opening up of the underlying assumptions of a secular society, the asking of the unasked questions, the probing of unrecognized presuppositions.[2]

This secular humanism I have here described is a third metanarrative (beyond that of Christianity and Islam) and it has exercised great influence all over the world. Secular humanism has its *be reshit*[3] and its alpha in naturalistic spontaneous generation and then naturalistic a-teleological[4] evolution, and its eschaton and omega in Gene Rodenberry's *Star Trek,* more or less.[5] People are enlightened, scientific, non-religious, tolerant, and live for the sake of learning and exploration.

I do not think secular modernity has much of a future though, which is why I will only touch on it from time to time. Suffice to say that the values of secular modernity have led to communities unwilling to perpetuate themselves by consistently producing enough humans to carry forth their cult. In other words, they just don't have enough kids for their form of life to have a long-term future. Indeed,

---

2   Newbigin, Lesslie (1989). *The Gospel in a Pluralist Society* (p. 220). Wm. B. Eerdmans Publishing Co.. Kindle Edition.

3   The Hebrew words with which the Bible opens: *in the beginning . . .*

4   A-teleological, meaning that this metanarrative may be able to answer questions like *what is it* and *what is it made of* but cannot answer questions about the *telos* (or final cause) of a thing, notably a human being: what is this here for? A chair is to be sat on, a television is for watching programs, and a human is for . . . what? Secular modernity cannot answer such questions beyond noting that we are here to reproduce and survive.

5   Understanding the world of Star Trek as the envisioned ideal future of secular humanism is not my original idea. I read it in Francis Gula's *The Good Life* (Paulist Press, 1999).

the words culture and cult are etymologically related, and with no common cult, there can be no culture, at least not over the long term. Meanwhile, it is devout and religious people—Jews, Christians, Muslims—that consistently produce offspring, witnessing to that ancient blessing on those who are fruitful and multiply.

But let us return to our main theme, that of comparing the metanarratives of Islam and Christianity. The word *metanarrative* is a combination of the common word for a story, *narrative*, with the Greek prefix *meta*. This prefix appears in other words, like metacarpal and metaphysics and metamorphosis, and means *after, beyond,* or *behind*. A narrative may be brief (your story of going to the grocery store), or it may be lengthy (the life of my hero, the Blessed Ramon Llull), or it may be sweeping and grand (the history of the Roman Empire). But a metanarrative is a story that stands behind *all* narratives in *all* places and claims to be able to account for them *all*, in their diversity of contexts, locations, and languages. Islam and Christianity propose such stories of everything—the narrative that lies *behind* or *beyond* all other narratives, even when the players are ignorant of its existence.

This book will compare Islam and Christianity as metanarratives—not primarily as religions. I believe this approach is more fruitful than that of "comparative religions." I will not treat themes topically—God, prophets, rituals, holy writings, etc. Rather, I will treat them chronologically, or better yet, narratively—as the story develops. Because these are stories of everything, they each propose that *your* own life is part of their metanarrative, and thereby demand that you make a decision and take a stand regarding how you relate to them.

I must start with a few caveats, though. First, this book is for non-specialists. This work can be well understood on its own, but a solid background in history and geography is helpful. A reading list is provided at the end of this book. Some of the vocabulary may not be familiar to the reader, so there are footnotes and a glossary.

Second, you will always be able to find an exception to what I am saying somewhere: there are Christians who do not baptize; there are Muslims who believe there were prophets after Muhammad. My purpose here is not to be exhaustive, but to describe in fairly grand sweeps how I understand these two metanarratives, based on years of living as a Christian among Muslims. All in all, though, I am trying to communicate the broad orthodoxy of Islam and Christianity, rather than propose radical new directions for them to take today or tell you what I think they should look like in the future.

Third, and finally, you will find many references to the Qur'an and the Bible. For the Bible I tend to use the English Standard Version, but don't use it exclusively. The Qur'an translations used are from Dawood, Pickthall, and Ali. Other translations I consulted were Khan, Arberry, and Shakir. When necessary, I translate the Arabic myself to aid in clarity.

One

PROTOLOGY

Protology is the study of beginnings. The Biblical and Qur'anic visions of Creation are, at a glance, similar. They both propose *ex nihilo*[1] creation by a single deity unopposed by other deities (as one finds in some other ancient creation narratives). In the Bible (Gen 1) creation unfolds gradually and in an orderly and progressive manner. The waters, which later in the Bible are symbols for danger and death as well as purification and rebirth, submit to God with no hint of resistance.

The Quran (which is about as long as the New Testament) does not contain as much detail, but the creative power of God is clear in that *he says be, and it is* (6:73). As in Genesis, Creation springs into being at God's verbal command. There is a difference, though, in the order of the days, as we read in the following hadith[2]:

> Abu Huraira reported that Allah's Messenger (pbuh) took hold of my hands and said: Allah the Exalted and Glorious, created the clay on Saturday and He created the mountains on Sunday and He created the trees on Monday and He created the things entailing labor on Tuesday and created light on Wednesday and He caused animals to spread on

---

1   *Ex Nihilo* means "Out of nothing."
2   A hadith is a narration of an event from the life of Muhammad or one of his companions. I should note that some historians recently have questioned the reliability of the hadiths, and even Muslims acknowledge that some hadiths are spurious fabrications.

Thursday and created Adam (pbuh) after 'Asr on Friday; the last creation at the last hour of the hours of Friday, ie. between afternoon and night.[3]

In the Bible we will learn later on that God created all things and that his Son is the firstborn of all Creation (Col 1:15), but this is to get ahead of ourselves. As we read Genesis 1 we have a similar protology to what the Qur'an describes—an omnipotent deity who speaks and Creates a universe *ex nihilo*. Furthermore, it is *good*. The created universe in its matter and physicality are good, and both metanarratives resist any tendency to think that matter (including the matter of the human flesh) is opposed to things spiritual.

Discussion Questions

In some ancient creation myths from the Middle East, Creation flows from a battle or conflict. What is the significance that in Islam and Christianity it does not?

If this is your first encounter with a hadith make sure to check out the word in the glossary. What do you think about the hadith? Do Christians have anything like them?

---

3   *Sahih Muslim* Number 6707, this is a reference to a hadith—see the glossary for more on this word.

Two

ANTHROPOLOGY: WHAT IS MAN?

Anthropology is the study of man. Within the context of our meta-narratives we now encounter the question: who is man and what is he here for?

Christianity

In Christianity, we find that God made man in his image and likeness, a teaching that is not present in the Qur'an. In the Bible there is the image of man being a crowning achievement, one who is *very good*. God shares his own sovereignty with this man by allowing him to name the animals. (Naming or renaming is an act that shows the power of one being over another.) It is not good for the man to be alone so he creates the female human. The female 'man' will not receive a name from the 'male' man until after they rebel against God, signifying that the male's need to rule over the female is not a part of the original 'good' plan of God, but is rather a symptom of their mutual alienation from God and, hence, from one another.

And now, let us turn to Genesis 3:

[1] Now the serpent was more crafty than any other beast of the field that the Lord God had made.

He said to the woman, "Did God actually say, 'You shall not eat of any tree in the garden'?" ² And the woman said to the serpent, "We may eat of the fruit of the trees in the garden, ³ but God said, 'You shall not eat of the fruit of the tree that is in the midst of the garden, neither shall you touch it, lest you die.'" ⁴ But the serpent said to the woman, "You will not surely die. ⁵ For God knows that when you eat of it your eyes will be opened, and you will be like God, knowing good and evil." ⁶ So when the woman saw that the tree was good for food, and that it was a delight to the eyes, and that the tree was to be desired to make one wise, she took of its fruit and ate, and she also gave some to her husband who was with her, and he ate. ⁷ Then the eyes of both were opened, and they knew that they were naked. And they sewed fig leaves together and made themselves loincloths.

⁸ And they heard the sound of the LORD God walking in the garden in the cool of the day, and the man and his wife hid themselves from the presence of the LORD God among the trees of the garden. ⁹ But the LORD God called to the man and said to him, "Where are you?" ¹⁰ And he said, "I heard the sound of you in the garden, and I was afraid, because I was naked, and I hid myself." ¹¹ He said, "Who told you that you were naked? Have you eaten of the tree of which I commanded you not to eat?" ¹² The man said, "The woman whom you gave to be with me, she gave me fruit of the tree, and I ate." ¹³ Then the LORD God said to the woman, "What is this that you have done?" The woman said, "The serpent deceived me, and I ate."

¹⁴ The LORD God said to the serpent, "Because you have done this, cursed are you above all livestock and above all beasts of the field; on your belly you shall go, and dust you shall eat all the days of your life. ¹⁵ I will put enmity between you and the woman, and between your offspring and her offspring; he shall bruise your head, and you shall bruise his heel."

¹⁶ To the woman he said, "I will surely multiply your pain in childbearing; in pain you shall bring forth children. Your desire shall be for your husband, and he shall rule over you."

¹⁷ And to Adam he said, "Because you have listened to the voice of your wife and have eaten of the tree of which I commanded you, 'You shall not eat of it,' cursed is the ground because of you; in pain you shall eat of it all the days of your life; ¹⁸ thorns and thistles it shall bring

forth for you; and you shall eat the plants of the field. [19] By the sweat of your face you shall eat bread, till you return to the ground, for out of it you were taken; for you are dust, and to dust you shall return."

[20] The man called his wife's name Eve, because she was the mother of all living. [21] And the LORD God made for Adam and for his wife garments of skins and clothed them.

[22] Then the LORD God said, "Behold, the man has become like one of us in knowing good and evil. Now, lest he reach out his hand and take also of the tree of life and eat, and live forever—" [23] therefore the LORD God sent him out from the garden of Eden to work the ground from which he was taken. [24] He drove out the man, and at the east of the garden of Eden he placed the cherubim and a flaming sword that turned every way to guard the way to the tree of life.

The garden narrative of Genesis builds up to the point where the male and female realize they are naked. First the setting of the Garden is introduced, followed by the snake, then the woman, then the man, and the realization that they are naked. After this apogee, God addresses the man, then the woman, and then unfolds the consequences of their rebellion beginning with an address to the snake, after which they are exiled from the Garden. The name for this sort of literary structure is *chiasm*. Here is a visual depiction of such a structure:

A. Garden
  B. Snake
    C. Woman
      D. Man
        X Naked
      D' Man
    C' Woman
  B' Snake
A' Exiled from Garden

In the Genesis passage we encounter three strategies by which the man and the woman attempt to avoid the truth—hiding from God, covering their own shame, and blaming others, including ultimately God ("The woman whom you gave to be with me . . ." in 3:12). But the gravity of this rebellion is revealed when man mercifully is exiled from Eden (Genesis 3:24) because otherwise they might live forever. That is, if they ate of the tree of life then they would have an eternal organic or biological life while living in perpetual alienation and spiritual death. All of Creation is corrupted because of this rebellion. Even the very agricultural patterns of the world are affected (Gen 3:17-19). The "man" human is alienated from the "woman" human, they are both alienated from God, and then the rest of nature is alienated from them too.

Death is the ultimate alienation unleashed into the world because the first man and woman (the crowning achievement of that universe), creatures that could *choose* to be in relation with God, chose to believe a lie. And that was what the serpent was proposing to the woman human, that God was basically a brat being selfish with his toys: he knows that you will not die, but in fact you can become like him (3:5). In saying this he was not blatantly lying: when they ate of the fruit they did not immediately physically die, as would be a plain reading of "for in the day that you eat of it you shall surely die" (2:17). And in a way they did become like God, knowing good from evil. But their knowledge of evil is a different kind of knowledge than that of God, because they know evil by becoming infected by its power. They know it because they are under its power, and because their offspring likewise will be under its power.

The tree was in reality a metaphysical necessity to safeguard and perpetuate the reality of free will, and the snake made it into a locus of suspicion. *Sin*, in its origin, is the misuse of our free will, where we choose to do something that we know is against God's law. But sin is only one symptom of death, and is not the fundamental problem. Through the misuse of freedom, death has entered into the entire universe that had been good. And so the stage is set: A good universe has been wounded. But not irrevocably damaged, we hope.

Islam

Unlike the Bible, the Qur'an gives a direct and unequivocal motive for God's creation of man: "We first created you [. . .] so that We might manifest to you Our power" (22:5).[1] With that in mind, let us turn to the Qur'anic narrative about Adam and Eve in surah 15.

Surahs in the Qur'an have their own context, like chapters from the Bible. The context of this surah (or chapter) of the Qur'an, which is titled *Al Hijr*, is the persistent rejection of Muhammad's message by most of his kinsfolk. In response to this rejection, Allah promises retribution upon these people, saying, "Again and again will those who disbelieve, wish that they had bowed (to Allah's will) in Islam" (15:2). Allah informs the Prophet that they would not have disbelieved unless he (Allah) had put disbelief in their hearts (15:12), and this is a just sentence because whenever Allah had sent them a messenger they ridiculed him (11). Moreover, even if a "Gate of Heaven" were clearly made visible to them, they would dismiss this divine portent with the excuse that a magical spell had been cast upon them (15). After some more comments about God's protection of heaven and its planets from devils, our attention is turned to how Allah has revealed himself to the universe by his Creation.

Here we find one of the main themes of the Qur'an, similar to what we find in the Bible: that the Creator has revealed some basic facts about himself in the grandeur and order of his Creation. In the context of this surah it can be understood as part of Allah's case against the people who will not submit to him and his Prophet—and Allah and Muhammad are completely inseparable in the Qur'an. The Qur'an is the psyche of Muhammad written large, as is all of Islam. Because God has revealed these basic realities about himself in the signs of nature, no one has an excuse to reject him or disbelieve.

But then we find the passage[2] that is of key interest to us, which I will treat as a running commentary:

> **26.** And indeed, We created man from sounding clay of altered black smooth mud.
> **27.** And the jinn, We created aforetime from the smokeless flame of fire.
> **28.** And (remember) when your Lord said to the angels: "I am going to create a man (Adam) from sounding clay of altered black smooth mud."

---

1   See 'Qur'an' and "Surah" in the glossary for an explanation of how the book is cited here.
2   And for this passage we will be using the translation of Mohsin Khan.

Here we have an introduction of three types of creatures that are part of God's Creation: humans, jinn, and angels. (There is not a consensus in Islamic thought about the devil, whether he is a rebellious angel or a jinn.)

> **29.** "So, when I have fashioned him completely and breathed into him (Adam) the soul which I created for him, then fall (you) down prostrating yourselves unto him."

Here we have a differentiation from the biblical narrative, which says nothing of angels in relation to the creation of man, though Job 38:7 would seem to indicate that there was a Hebrew belief that angels existed before or at the time of Creation. In the Qur'an, though, God desires for the angels to bow before man in order to demonstrate that man is in some way superior to the angels.

> **30.** So, the angels prostrated themselves, all of them together.
> **31.** Except *Iblis* (the devil), - he refused to be among the prostrators.
> **32.** (Allah) said: "O *Iblis*! What is your reason for not being among the prostrators?"
> **33.** (*Iblis*) said: "I am not the one to prostrate myself to a human being, whom You created from sounding clay of altered black smooth mud."

We start to get the feeling here that the Creation narrative is more about the antagonism between Satan and God, rather than the overarching state of man in relation to God. Satan will not pay homage to man because he regards him as inferior—apparently, he thinks that a spiritual being is superior to the man, an embodied and physical being.

> **34.** (Allah) said: "Then, get out from here, for verily, you are *Rajim* (an outcast or a cursed one)."
> **35.** "And verily, the curse shall be upon you till the Day of Recompense (i.e. the Day of Resurrection)."
> **36.** (*Iblis*) said: "O my Lord! Give me then respite till the Day they (the dead) will be resurrected."
> **37.** Allah said: "Then, verily, you are of those reprieved,
> **38.** "Till the Day of the time appointed."

Satan asks for reprieve from God and this is granted to him, until the day of the resurrection. In the Bible we don't have Satan asking for reprieve, but we do have Satan, in the book of Job, conversing with God in heaven.[3] It is not until the eschaton that Satan[4] and his devils (in Christianity) are cast into the Lake of Fire (Revelation 21).

> **39.** (*Iblis*) said: "O my Lord! Because you misled me, I shall indeed adorn the path of error for them (mankind) on the earth, and I shall mislead them all. **40.** Except Your chosen, (guided) slaves among them."
> **41.** (Allah) said: "This is the Way which will lead straight to Me."
> **42.** "Certainly, you shall have no authority over My slaves, except those who follow you of the *Ghawin* (associators, those who go astray, criminals, polytheists, and evil-doers, etc.). **43.** And surely, Hell is the promised place for them all."

Iblis (possibly a corruption of the Greek *diabolos*) declares his enmity to God and his created humans, vowing to lead them all astray, excepting the believers whom God chooses to guide. In typical Qur'anic style the narrative then becomes an occasion for warning the hearers regarding the fires of hell.

We also find another narrative in the longest surah of the Qur'an, The Cow. This is the beginning point for most people reading the Qur'an from beginning to end, as it is the second chapter in the Qur'an after the brief opening prayer.

In surah 2:31-37 we find a few more things about man, and I want to highlight two of them. Man is vice-regent of God, and the basic goodness of man is not spoiled by the sin of Adam and his wife. There is also a point worth mentioning about the angels in this chapter: they are suspicious of man at his creation, asking if humans will not spread mischief throughout the world. God's answer to them is enigmatic, simply saying that he knows what the angels do not know. We also find in the Qur'anic narrative that the expulsion from paradise is temporary, and that man may one day return.

---

3   It is worth noting that in Job we technically have "the satan," meaning, "the accuser."
4   Note that in Islam 'satan' is not a proper noun, and refers in general to what Christians would call demons. *Iblis*, on the other hand, refers to one specific being.

Adam and Eve repent of their error, are forgiven, and that concludes the drama of the Garden. God in the Qur'an does not need an atoning sacrifice. He can simply forgive them, and their basic moral integrity is preserved. Since humans are basically good, they are born in a right relationship with God and nature. In other words, they are born in a state of Islam or *submission* to Allah.[5] This helps us understand why Muslims insist that Islam is the natural religion, and that it is only through incorrect instruction that children unwittingly leave Islam as they are taught the doctrines of Christianity or Judaism or secularism. Moreover, this is why people who convert to Islam as adults don't call themselves "converts" but "reverts," having returned to the relation they (and we) were all born into: Islam.

Let that sink in for a moment: according to the Islamic metanarrative *you* were born a Muslim, and the only reason you are not still a Muslim is that you are ignorant of God's will and susceptible to the work of the devil, Iblis.

An analogy

Imagine a person who is having some symptoms and not feeling well, and he visits two doctors. One tells the man to get some rest, eat better, and exercise more. The other one tells the man that his condition is terminal, and that there is nothing at all the man can do to save himself from death. These two doctors correspond to the two anthropologies (theories of humanity) above.

Because the two movements understand the fundamental problem differently, everything else develops differently in the subsequent moves. If it is true that humans are basically good, and that the problem is that they are simply not fully aware of God's benevolent will for life (the *shari'a*), then the solution of sending down an infallible and clear book is a good one. If, on the other hand, the very nature of the human as a moral being

---

5   I have heard people say that the Arabic word *Islam* translates to the English word *peace*. That is patently incorrect. What can be said is that the Arabic word for peace (*salam*) is grammatically related to the Arabic word for submission (*Islam*), in that both have the some root of *s-l-m*.

has been compromised, then no matter how clear God's directions may be, it will not suffice. This is because humans, even knowing what is right, will sometimes, maybe quite often, not do it. Also, if God can simply opt for mercy rather than justice in his sovereign power (as in the Qur'an) then the notion of a sacrifice made by God on behalf of man (as when God kills the animal to cover man's nakedness in Genesis 3) is unnecessary and bizarre. In Islam, when Adam and his wife are forgiven, the relation is restored. In the Genesis narrative, however, their attempt to cover their own shame (the fig leaves) fails, and God himself must step in and shed the blood of an animal in order to provide them with animal skins. It is those garments, provided by the Creator, that are able to conceal their shame.

This, I propose, is the fundamental bifurcation between Islam and Christianity. It is right there in the anthropology and specifically the hamartiology (theory of sin). God, whatever he may be like, is responding to this foundational problem—a problem *not* of his own making. Another way of saying this is that one must understand the *bad news* before they understand the *good news*. If a person doesn't believe that they are a sinner who, of their own resources, is unable to reach out to and obey God, then the message that Jesus died for them is nonsensical.

There is a technical word here we should learn: *concupiscence.* I learned this word while studying moral theology from an old Marianist priest and I have found it to be a very helpful term in comparing Islam and Christianity. This term refers to an innate tendency towards doing what is not good, and all humans share this. This word helps us to understand the mystery of human-ness: that we are capable of such good and beautiful things while also being capable of immense, intentional harm and evil. God created us good, and will one day restore us to that goodness. But for the time being we are now compromised and unable to, of our own resources, reach out to him. I don't think that Islam has a satisfactory way of explaining this reality: that humans are, as creatures of God, good but that even when we know the rules (think Ten Commandments) we don't always follow them. Even when we know what we are doing is actually harmful to ourselves (e.g., an affair, an addiction), we often do it anyway, regardless of the consequences.

Before ending this chapter, we must explore how God starts to respond to these two different foundational problems, or two different versions of the bad news. In Christianity, it is called death. Death has entered into the universe and in terms of our own spiritual death and our interconnectedness with each other as humans (unlike the angels, each of which is his own species), we call this original sin. This death has biological facets–the corruption of the human body, and the inevitability of aging and dying—but the immediate effect is spiritual and relational.

In Islam there is a theory (or hamartiology) of original innocence, unlike Christianity's hamartiology of original sin. According to this theory, you and I were born like Adam and the female were created—in a state of innocence before and submission to the Creator. Consequently, each person will stand alone before God and perhaps they will be forgiven, perhaps they will not. They can hope he will be merciful, but for most people there is no way to be certain.

Discussion Questions

The author emphasizes that the key problem in the Christian meta-narrative is death, and that sin is simply one effect of death. Have you ever heard this before? Do you think it is correct? What are the implications of this interpretation?

Islam proposes that a key facet of the human dilemma is ignorance. Do you agree or not? Is this not the general belief of people in the West?

"Sin: this is the misuse of our own free will . . ." Free will seems to be a controversial issue in various Christian denominations. Does that affect this primary distinction with Islam?

Re-read the analogy at the end of the chapter. Is it helpful? Do you think it is accurate?

Three

ISRAEL, A FAILED ATTEMPT

So how does God respond to these two problems in our competing metanarratives? In Islam, there is ignorance or *jahiliyya*—people do not know the ordinances of God. In Christianity the complex problem of death has entered the universe, corrupting nature, relationships, and the human soul. This is now the time to explore the question of Israel, which has a prominent role in both the Bible and the Quran.

Christianity

In Christianity, we encounter the mystery of *election*.[1] God chooses Abram and decides to make a great nation of him, promising to bless all the peoples of the earth through him and his seed.[2] This mystery of election refers to God's choice of individuals for certain saving works and we rarely find a clear reason for this choice. Indeed, God often chooses the most unlikely person for his great works (Muslims would probably agree with this, pointing to God's choice of an illiterate Prophet). Why Abram? Why Mary? We are not certain. Sometimes we can guess: Why Moses? Because he had been brought up within Pharaoh's household. But why Jacob? And

---

1   See *election* in the glossary.
2   Gen 12:1-3

for heaven's sake, why Peter to be the head Apostle? He seems to be a poor candidate for such a leadership role.

We don't know. But this is part of God's character in the Bible. The God of the Bible does not appear anxious to explain the working of his will to the reader, but we do find the following dynamic always at work: election is always for the sake of the other. Abraham is chosen for the blessing of the peoples of the earth; Mary is chosen to give birth to the Messiah who will be the savior for his people and a light to the gentiles; Peter is chosen so he can strengthen his brothers; and so on.

God chooses Abram and this is the beginning of God's plan (in the Bible) to address the central problem of our story, which is the entry of death into the universe. God will use Abram as a conduit for his blessing, telling him that in him all the peoples of earth would be blessed. Under the rubric of blessing God will begin to triumph over death. God expresses his power over Abram and Sarai by renaming them Abraham and Sarah. God renews his covenant with Isaac, and then God chooses Jacob over Esau. Jacob, in one of the most baffling passages in the Bible,[3] contends with the Angel of the Lord before crossing over the stream named Jabbok. Because of this, Jacob, like his grandfather, is renamed, and receives the mysterious name Israel, one who struggles with El (God). God has chosen to use this sort of man—one who struggles against him but also for him (in order to receive his blessing), and who struggles against man but also for man.

The descendants of Israel end up settling in Egypt, and then the God of their fathers sends Moses; the God of the Hebrews contends with the gods of the Egyptians and emerges victorious. The Israelites are delivered from Egypt and worship the Lord at the foot of Sinai where God reveals his Torah to Moses.

Why does he do all these things? It might seem that this jives better with the Islamic narrative: People don't know his rules, and at Sinai he is going to tell them those rules. The problem is solved.

But this is not the answer we find in the Hebrew Scriptures. What was God's strategy here? How does the election of Israel further his plan to see his blessing spread to all peoples through Abraham? We turn to Isaiah 2:1–5 to better understand the purpose of Israel's election:

---

3   Gen 32

¹ The word that Isaiah the son of Amoz saw concerning Judah and Jerusalem. ² It shall come to pass in the latter days that the mountain of the house of the LORD shall be established as the highest of the mountains, and shall be lifted up above the hills; and all the nations shall flow to it, ³ and many peoples shall come, and say: "Come, let us go up to the mountain of the LORD, to the house of the God of Jacob, that he may teach us his ways and that we may walk in his paths." For out of Zion shall go the law, and the word of the LORD from Jerusalem. ⁴ He shall judge between the nations, and shall decide disputes for many peoples; and they shall beat their swords into plowshares, and their spears into pruning hooks; nation shall not lift up sword against nation, neither shall they learn war anymore. ⁵ O house of Jacob, come, let us walk in the light of the LORD.

God desires to have a people so unique in everything they do—what they eat, how they dress, how they rest, the place they worship, that they have no king, and so on—that the surrounding nations⁴ would be attracted to their way of life and would voluntarily go up to Zion to learn this Torah. And so, the blessing of God would spread from Abraham through Israel to the ends of the earth and to the entire earth. This blessing counteracts and can overcome the multi-faceted problem of death.

This plan (apparently) fails: After the reign of Solomon ten of the twelve tribes depart from the confederation and become their own kingdom, called Israel. The large tribe of Judah with some folks from the tribes of Benjamin and Levi (which did not get a chunk of land, but was scattered throughout the kingdom) remain with Jerusalem as their main city. This split takes place around 921 BC. The Kingdom of Israel in the north is exiled by the Assyrians around 720 BC and their ethnic and religious particularity is largely lost. The southern Kingdom of Judah remains for a while longer, but is finally conquered and exiled in the 580's BC to Babylon, which is then conquered by Persia, in today's Iran. Eventually, the

---

4   The *nations* or *peoples* are a recurring theme throughout the whole of the Bible's plan of salvation: in the Abrahamic Covenant God says that he will, through Abraham, bless all the *peoples* or *nations* of the earth. The Mosaic Covenant represents the election of Israel to be a *holy people* or *holy nation*. Later, after the sealing of the New Covenant, Jesus commands his apostles to go to *all nations*. Finally, the culmination of human history has members from *every tribe and tongue and nation* worshiping God in unison.

Jews[5] are given permission to return and rebuild Jerusalem, its walls, and the Temple. A couple of intrepid leaders like Nehemiah and Ezra lead this effort, though most of the Jews remain in Babylon, where many of them prosper.[6] It is among this group of returnees that we find the ministry of Haggai, who must be the most successful prophet in the whole Bible, because after one brief sermon admonishing the people to rebuild the Temple, they promptly do so—even if it is a pale comparison to the first Temple. But the Davidic dynasty no longer rules over a sovereign, independent kingdom. There is a period of time when the Hasmoneans pull this off, but it is a fleeting dream.

There were instances of the gentiles knowing the true God through Israel's witness—Ruth the Moabite, the queen of Sheba, Naaman the Syrian are all examples. But on the whole, the vision of Isaiah 2 has not come to pass: the nations of the earth have not seen the holiness, blessing, and uniqueness of Israel. God's election of Israel for the sake of the nations has been stymied by the Israelites lack of faithfulness to the Torah. The vision of Isaiah 2 has failed. It appears that God's plan in his election of Israel has failed and that God's blessing to all nations, promised to Abraham, has not come to pass.

Islam

Now let us return to the Qur'anic vision, which likewise ends up in apparent failure and then figures out how to fix the problem.

The Qur'an does not contain lengthy historical-theological texts like Samuel, Kings, Chronicles, Ezra and Nehemiah. While it addresses Jews from time to time, it is not *fundamentally* concerned with Jews like the Bible is. But we can outline some key points that will help us understand the theology of history that undergirds Islam.

First, there is the belief that Allah has sent messengers with his guidance to peoples all around the world. We know the names of some of them—many in the Bible, but not all. But most of these names are pre-

---

5   It is finally at this point in history—the exile—that we can speak of *Jews*, rather than Hebrews or Israelites or Judahites.

6   Scholars of this community in Babylon produced the Babylonian Talmud, generally considered superior to the Jerusalem Talmud.

sumably totally unknown to us today. Think of the Mongols, the Aztecs, the Cheyenne, the Samburu, the Mayans—according to the Qur'an, Allah sent them messengers. Allah has been active in informing ignorant humans about how to worship him and informing them of right and wrong:

> [O Muhammad], We have revealed Our will to you as We revealed it to Noah and to the prophets who came after him; as we revealed it to Abraham, Ishmael, Isaac, Jacob, and the tribes; to Jesus, Job, Jonah, Aaron, Solomon and David, to whom we gave the Psalms. Of some apostles We have already told you, but there are others of whom We have not yet spoken (God spoke directly to Moses): apostles who brought good news to mankind and admonished them, so that they might have no plea against God after their coming. God is mighty and wise. (4:163–165, Dawood translation; see also 6:42–45)

Second, some of these messengers have even received messages that were written down. To the Israelites God sent men like Moses, David, and Jesus, and their messages were recorded in the Torah, the Psalms, and the Gospels. However, there is a strong tradition in Islam proposing that the texts of those books were corrupted.[7] Which is to say that the Torah, Psalms, and Gospels you have are *not* the genuine messages God gave to Moses, David, and Jesus. In the Muslim mind, there were once valid, revealed texts of the Torah, Psalms, and Gospels, but they no longer exist today.

Two points should be mentioned here: not all Muslims believe this (although in my experience most do), and this doctrine is *not in the Qur'an*.[8] But when we talk about metanarrative, the paramount concern is not textual, critical, historical truth, but what the communities *perceive* to be that truth. In other words, it doesn't matter that the Qur'an doesn't explicitly say that the texts are corrupted, or, for that matter, that Jesus was not crucified.[9] That the Israelites received so many prophets yet do not accept

---

7   See *corruption* in the glossary.
8   Some people will reference passages like 2:75, 79; 3:78 and 5:13–14. But note that these do not allege a corruption of the text of the revealed books, but only how they are read or interpreted by the Jews.
9   4:157 simply says that *Jews* did not crucify him, which is of course correct, because the Romans did.

the revelation to Muhammad marks them as a problematic group in the Qur'an.

Third, that Allah has built into his Creation signs that witness to monotheism (rather than polytheism) and his power and wisdom. The argument in the Qur'an is that the person who is attendant to these *signs* (an important term in the Qur'an) will know these things. The astute observer of nature should be able to figure these things out without a prophet or messenger from God. This notion, that God reveals things about himself in Creation, is called natural revelation. Following is an example of how the Qur'an handles these issues:

> Lo! In the creation of the heavens and the earth, and the difference of
> night and day, and the ships which run upon the sea with that which
> is of use to men, and the water which Allah sendeth down from the
> sky, thereby reviving the earth after its death, and dispersing all kinds
> of beasts therein, and (in) the ordinance of the winds, and the clouds
> obedient between heaven and earth: are signs (of Allah's Sovereignty)
> for people who have sense. (2:164, Pickthall)

All in all, the metanarrative of Islam is trying to address the problem of *jahiliyya* (ignorance): people are not aware of God's will for society. They may know some basic things because they were born Muslims and are basically good. But there are parts of the natural moral order that humans do not know: they do not know that women should cover their hair; they do not know that they should pray five times a day; they do not know that pork is not food; they do not know that angels will not enter houses with statues or dogs; they do not know how to wear their beard and how to dress; they do not know how to divide the spoils of war or inheritance for children; and so on. God sent messengers and prophets to teach these things, but the actual content of those messages is either unknown to us or the texts have been corrupted.

Some people have proposed that there is a fundamental commonality because of one of the key prophets of Judaism, Christianity, and Islam: Abraham. So, at this point I need to address the idea of Abrahamic faiths, and the trope, "We all go back to Abraham who is the father of faith." This sounds very nice and serves an important psychological purpose in that it comforts Christians and Jews who are alarmed by the reality of Islamic terrorism. Tracing the three faiths back to Abraham and proposing a common source implies that, in spite of the reality of proliferating Islamic terrorism today, there is a deep commonality and so we should not even entertain the position that the terrorism is authentically Islamic. The problem with this theory is not hard to identify though: the Abraham in the Qur'an is not the same as the Abraham in the Bible.

When the Jew or Christian reads about Abraham in Genesis, there is a good chance that his Muslim interlocutor thinks that his Genesis narrative is from a corrupt, untrustworthy version of the original, lost Torah.[10] This is not the place to offer a detailed comparative study of Abraham in the three faiths, but I do want to clarify that the Abraham of the Bible is not identical to the Abraham of the Qur'an. Two differences are worthy of note: in the Qur'an it is Ishmael, not Isaac, that is taken up the mountain to be sacrificed; and Abraham is the person who built the Ka'ba,[11] which is the large cube which is circumambulated[12] by Muslims during their pilgrimage (hajj).

Conclusion

In both metanarratives you end up with a similar sense of failure regarding Israel. In other words, Judaism has failed. This people privileged with an abundance of messengers and prophets, including Jesus, has not lived up to its potential:

And remember Allah took a Covenant from the People of the Book, to make it known and clear to mankind, and not to hide it . . . (3:187, Yusuf Ali)

---

10   In my experience, a Muslim will rarely tell you that he thinks your book is not trustworthy, because he is used to treating the artifacts of other religions with respect and because he wants to offer a positive image of Islam to non-Muslims. This is all the more the case in the West, where Muslims are very aware that many people (religious and non-religious) are pretty wary of Islam.

11   Qur'an 2:125

12   That is, they walk around it

It was the duty of the Jews and the Christians to make known this revelation to all mankind, but they had not done so.[13]

Discussion Questions

The author proposes that election of individual humans is not primarily related to the salvation of those individuals, but God's desire to save all of humanity. Do you agree or not? What biblical verses have you heard to bolster the idea that God elected certain humans before Creation to be saved, while not electing others?

Page 18 talks about 'Abrahamic faiths.' Have you ever heard this phrase? What does it mean? The author is critical of the use of the phrase, why is that? Do you find his argument to be compelling or weak?

After reading this chapter has your opinion regarding Israel in the Bible changed at all? How so? Why or why not?

---

13 It is worth asking, what if Christians had actually been diligent in evangelizing the Arabian Peninsula? What if Muhammad had encountered a vibrant Christian community in that city and in Yathrib?

Four

JESUS, THE MEDIATOR BETWEEN GOD AND MAN

Both metanarratives propose that God responds with a sort of arch-representative to the two problems—death in Christianity, and ignorance in Islam. In both metanarratives this arch-representative goes on to found a specific community with a particular mission and way of life that define the genius and spirit of that community, even to this day. In this chapter we will examine the arch-representative of God in the Christian metanarrative—Jesus. In the following chapter we will explore the arch-representative of the divine will in Islam—Muhammad.

Christianity proposes that the foundational problem is death. Cancer, crime, divorce, child abuse, wars, human trafficking, addiction, war, abuse of the earth and its resources, depression, natural disasters—all of these are symptoms of this one, single problem. Sin is a manifestation of death, and through the commission of a sin death was brought into the universe, but the problem is deeper than sin. Death is the foundational issue to be addressed in the Christian metanarrative.

Jesus believes he has an answer for this problem. In the synoptic Gospels it is the Kingdom of God, and in the Gospel of John it is summed up in the one Greek word *zoe*, which means life. This is the word on Jesus' tongue when he says he is the resurrection and the life, and that he had come that they might have abundance of life. This is the word in John 3:16 that explains that whosoever believes in Jesus will not perish, but have everlasting life. Everlasting life meaning the life of God, as opposed to mere and temporary biological life, which has its own Greek word, *bios.*

Jesus really had one overarching topic he taught throughout the Gospels: the Kingdom of God, or the Reign of God. You don't find Jesus ever using the word *grace*; you have him saying the word "church" only twice in the Gospels (both in Matthew). He also doesn't talk about dying and going to heaven in the way we normally think about it. So why does he talk about the Kingdom of God (or Kingdom of Heaven, in Matthew)? He talks about the Kingdom of God in relation to the final judgment (like in the parable of the net), he talks about it in relation to money (the widow's mite, the parable of the shrewd servant), in relation to rejoicing at the repentance of sinner (the so-called parable of the prodigal son, which should be called the parable of the son in the field).

In some ways Jesus was a very conventional teacher: having followers and talking about the Kingdom of God and the Torah—these were typical activities for a Jewish teacher in the 1st Century. But he did differ from other 1st century Jewish teachers. He chose his own followers; he taught that the Torah could only be rightly lived out and interpreted in the light of the Kingdom of God, as when he healed on the Sabbath, or as when the impure woman was healed by touching the hem of his garment rather than Jesus being defiled by her impurity; and he spoke on his own authority.[1] He also claimed some divine prerogatives, like forgiving people's sins. His vision was to see God's reign—one of forgiveness, compassion, healing for the nations—advance into this world. This world's conquest by the Kingdom of God would address the problem of death, because the power of the heavenly kingdom of eternal and spiritual life would vanquish the power of death. Ultimately, the locus of the Kingdom of God is in the person of Jesus himself and his actual, physical body. This is why the Gospel of John focuses so much on Jesus' seven "I am" statements: it is impossible to understand the Kingdom of God and its nature without understanding Jesus himself. This is also, I suspect, why his disciples must actually eat his flesh and drink his blood (John 6). Indeed, it is impossible to enter the

---

1   For more on Jesus in his own historical context see the early chapters of David Bosch's *Transforming Mission* (Orbis, 2011) and Kenneth Bailey's *Jesus through Middle Eastern Eyes* (IVP Academic, 2009).

Kingdom of God apart from acceptance of the reality that Jesus is the Lord in this Kingdom.

The most rudimentary form of the proclamation of the Gospel was "The time is fulfilled, and the kingdom of God is at hand; repent and believe in the gospel" (Mark 1:15). The reign of God, or day of the Lord, was coming and John the Baptist's Jewish audience knew what that would look like: "Behold, the day of the LORD comes, cruel, with wrath and fierce anger, to make the land a desolation and to destroy its sinners from it" (Is 13:9).

The good news is that people can prepare for this Day of Judgment that is coming: they can prepare by repenting, and then demonstrate this repentance by being baptized. This was good news indeed!

The word *evangel* or *gospel* was not unfamiliar to the people of the 1st Century in the Roman Empire. When there was good news from the emperor—if he had won a major battle—then an evangelist would come to the cities and announce that good news. That one can be saved from the wrath of God by repenting is great news!

Jesus mostly referred to himself as the Son of Man. People often believe he used this title because he wanted to emphasize his solidarity with the rest of humanity, but this interpretation is incorrect. The title appears to come from Daniel 7:

> I saw in the night visions, and behold, with the clouds of heaven there came one like a son of man, and he came to the Ancient of Days and was presented before him. And to him was given dominion and glory and a kingdom, that all peoples, nations, and languages should serve him; his dominion is an everlasting dominion, which shall not pass away, and his kingdom one that shall not be destroyed. (Dan 7:13-14)

The Son of Man is unlike any other human as he receives dominion directly from God. It is not a dominion over the land of Israel, but all the earth, and unlike a Davidic king, his reign does not end upon his death, but is an everlasting reign. Jesus, in choosing this title for himself, is emphasizing that he is the holder of dominion and power in the Kingdom of God which he is announcing. Moreover, his kingdom is indeed over Israel, but it is expanded to include *all people, nations, and languages* (note that recurring theme of the nations).

So why did Jesus get killed? This is a fascinating question in my mind. Mostly he was up in the region of Galilee (northern Israel, today). He taught people, healed them, and cast out demons—all indications that God's reign was coming into this world. So what got him killed?

In many ways, Jesus resembled the Pharisees, who were also concerned with the Law of God and the Kingdom of God.[2] They were also lay people rather than professional scribes or priests. Jesus ate with some of them, when he was going to Jerusalem some of them warned him not to go. We know, from the book of Acts, that a number of Pharisees became Christians. But there was one key point where Jesus and the Pharisees disagreed: the nature of the Kingdom of God.

Most first century Jews believed they had a pretty good grasp on the Kingdom of God: God would someday send a man from the line of David, from the tribe of Judah, who would through military expertise expel the Romans and reestablish a sovereign kingdom. Jesus had a much broader vision of the nature of the Kingdom of God. For those who entered into it and lived according to its laws, it was healing and salvation and forgiveness. For those who opposed it, it was judgment and led to an outer darkness.[3] Moreover, the Kingdom of God has a priority over the Torah. Jesus' teaching and his miracles indicate a disagreement over the correct interpretation and application of Torah, and this was the key difference he had with some Pharisees. In short, for Jesus the coming of the Kingdom of God was the main event and Torah obedience was subservient to it—the Torah needed to be read and interpreted through the lens of the coming Kingdom.

In the so-called parable of the prodigal son we find this point elucidated very well. If you read the beginning of the chapter (Lk 14) you get the context for it: that some Pharisees are complaining about Jesus because of the company he keeps. This is the occasion for his parable and the Pharisees are the audience. In this parable the father's house is the locus of the Kingdom of God. The son who left and squandered his inheritance is

---

2   I am indebted to the Rev. David Pileggi of Christ Church in the Old City of Jerusalem for these insights regarding the similarities of Jesus' and the Pharisees' religious vocations.

3   Which I understand as a perpetual and absolute ontological solitude: an unnatural universe created by one's self for one's self in which the self is the only object of worship, and wherein *do as thou wilt shall be the whole of the law.*

like the whore or tax collector—he was very far from God's Kingdom. He repented and returned to the home, and his father ran out, in joy, to meet him, and bring him into the house. The son in the field corresponds to the Pharisees. The father goes out to see him and asks, *Why does he not come into the house?* The father explains by making two important points: that rejoicing is the appropriate response (not grumbling, as the Pharisees were doing at first); and that the younger son *has no inheritance*—he already spent it. The son in the field will inherit everything he has, but he needs to come into the house. The parable ends with no resolution, because it is up to the grumbling Pharisees to decide if they are going to rejoice and enter the house, or stay in the field grumbling.[4]

By the last week of his life in Jerusalem (Holy Week), it seems that time is up for them to repent and enter the house. Jesus tells them one of his most incendiary parables about a man who had a vineyard and then left it in the trust of some servants, who turn out to be wicked and kill the owner's messengers and then even his son. Jesus concludes that the owner will come back to the vineyard and "put those wretches to a miserable death" (Mt 21:41) and then rent the vineyard out to others. The audience here is not only some Pharisees but also some of the chief priests, who under normal circumstances were bitter enemies.

Returning to the main point, Jesus' message about the Kingdom of God was very original, even scandalous, and made him powerful enemies. Also, the very word "kingdom" was just political enough that it could be twisted into a charge of insurrection against Caesar. The punishment for this was crucifixion, and it was important that the execution of Jesus be carried out by Romans lest any Jews become ritually impure on the Passover by killing a man.

Another key factor that led to the crucifixion of Jesus was his rhetoric about the Temple. Jesus did not spend most of his time in Jerusalem, but he managed to make powerful enemies there anyway. When he foretold the destruction of the Temple and then claimed that he himself, in his very

---

4   By way of application, most Christians who have been going to church for most of their lives are like the son in the field, and they are challenged to rejoice when someone repents and enters into the Church, rather than grumble about it. Regarding the parable of the lost sheep, they should ask if they are willing to be left alone for a while with the other 98 sheep, so the pastor can go out and get that lost sheep.

body, was the real and genuine Temple, the priests and Sadducees (centered in Jerusalem) reasonably felt threatened. The Temple was, after all, the source of their power and wealth. When he cleansed the court of the Gentiles in the Temple from the moneychangers, he was likewise making an important point—not about capitalism or greed so much, but about the gentiles. The Temple was supposed to be a house of prayer *for all nations*, not just Jews.[5] That was the reason for having a court of the gentiles, that the vision of Isaiah 2:1-5 might be fulfilled. Yet instead of welcoming in the nations to know the one true God, the Temple authorities had allocated the space for commerce.

But Jesus is very popular! The Jews who welcomed him into Jerusalem on Palm Sunday did not suddenly turn on him during Holy Week. Indeed, one of the main problems for those who would arrest Jesus was that he was always in public, surrounded by scores of people who respected and loved him. And so, he is arrested while praying in a garden.

But the crucifixion does not come as a surprise to Jesus. He knows this is coming because he has identified himself with the figure of the suffering servant in Isaiah. The conflation of the figure of the Son of Man from Daniel 7 and then the suffering servant from Isaiah is fascinating. They would appear to be very different figures, but Jesus is both the victorious Son of Man *and* the despised Servant. Isaiah 53 is a fine example of the work and life of the Servant:

Who has believed what he has heard from us? And to whom has the arm of the LORD been revealed? For he grew up before him like a young plant, and like a root out of dry ground; he had no form or majesty that we should look at him, and no beauty that we should desire him. He was despised and rejected by men; a man of sorrows, and acquainted with grief; and as one from whom men hide their faces he was despised, and we esteemed him not. Surely he has borne our griefs and carried our sorrows; yet we esteemed him stricken, smitten by God, and afflicted. But he was pierced for our transgressions; he was crushed for our iniquities; upon him was the chastisement that brought us peace, and with his wounds we are healed. All we like sheep have gone astray;

---

5   Note the presence of the *nations* again.

we have turned—every one—to his own way; and the LORD has laid on him the iniquity of us all. He was oppressed, and he was afflicted, yet he opened not his mouth; like a lamb that is led to the slaughter, and like a sheep that before its shearers is silent, so he opened not his mouth. By oppression and judgment he was taken away; and as for his generation, who considered that he was cut off out of the land of the living, stricken for the transgression of my people? And they made his grave with the wicked and with a rich man in his death, although he had done no violence, and there was no deceit in his mouth. Yet it was the will of the LORD to crush him; he has put him to grief; when his soul makes an offering for guilt, he shall see his offspring; he shall prolong his days; the will of the LORD shall prosper in his hand. Out of the anguish of his soul he shall see and be satisfied; by his knowledge shall the righteous one, my servant, make many to be accounted righteous, and he shall bear their iniquities. (Is 53:1-11)

This passage helps us to understand why Jesus can say things like, "For even the Son of Man came not to be served but to serve, and to give his life as a ransom for many" (Mk 10:45), and why John the Baptist can exclaim, "Behold, the lamb of God, who takes away the sins of the world!" (Jn 1:29)

Here is where we understand the centrality of the Cross. The Cross is God's solution to our guilt before him. The Cross provides an atoning covering, so God can be both just and merciful at the same time without appearing arbitrary. It is the resurrection, however, that is the beginning of the new Creation. The old Creation is suffused with the cancer of death, but Jesus' resurrection body belongs to the New Creation, as if it belonged to a different and new universe. This is why it can do things normal bodies can't (like walk through walls) and why people who know him don't recognize him at first. His body itself is the life, it is the Temple, and he himself is Israel.

He himself is Israel? Did he say that? The answer is clearly yes. One of the primary metaphors for the relationship between God and Israel in the Old Testament is that Israel is God's vine or vineyard: "You brought a vine out of Egypt; you drove out the nations and planted it. You cleared the ground for it; it took deep root and filled the land. The mountains were covered with its shade, the mighty cedars with its branches. It sent out its branches to the sea and its shoots to the River" (Ps 80:8-11). We also see this imagery in Isaiah 5.

But in John 15 Jesus says that he himself is "the true vine" and that "If anyone does not abide in me, he is thrown away as a branch." Why is this important? Because it reveals that God's election of Israel was in fact not a failure. The true Israel of God is this single man—Jesus. He himself in his body has reconstituted Israel. The history of Israel reaches its apogee and fulfillment in this single person and anyone who abides in him is indeed abiding in the Israel of God and is a branch of that true vine.

Matthew understood this and is making a similar point when he takes Hosea 11:1 radically out of context to refer to the return of the Holy Family from Egypt. Hosea 11:1–4 reads:

> When Israel was a child, I loved him, and out of Egypt I called my son. The more they were called, the more they went away; they kept sacrificing to the Baals and burning offerings to idols. Yet it was I who taught Ephraim to walk; I took them up by their arms, but they did not know that I healed them. I led them with cords of kindness, with the bands of love, and I became to them as one who eases the yoke on their jaws, and I bent down to them and fed them.

This passage is obviously a historical recollection of the Exodus and God's son is Israel. But Matthew (2:15) quotes this verse to refer to Jesus. Matthew knows very well what the original verse is about, but he now believes that Jesus himself *is* the Israel of God. Hosea's perception of the meaning was partial, because, as Matthew knows, Jesus *is* Israel. The precise word here is reconstitution: Jesus is reconstituting Israel. He is doing this on purpose, too, and his choice of twelve disciples is yet one more indication of this.

Is this replacement theology? No, it is not; it is fulfillment theology. There is no question of Israel being the people of God, and they are not being "replaced" by the Church—a Church which would quickly become majority-gentile. Rather, this understanding of Israel is focused on Jesus Christ himself, because he was deeply concerned with explaining to his disciples who he was and what his relation to his Father was. Whatever ethnic Israel was, it reached its climax and summation in this one person—its Temple, its Torah, the Davidic monarchy, and its twelve tribes. God's promise of the Land to Israel is not cancelled, but expanded and universalized in Jesus.[6] He is the Son of Man who is given dominion over all the earth, not just a small strip of land in southwest Asia. Also, because Jesus' gathering of followers (called the Church) is no longer closely identified with one ethnic group, he is "a light for the nations" (Is 42:6).

In the beginning of this book I complained that the word *religion* is so misunderstood as to be harmful. But we are now at a point where we can rightly understand the word in its historical context. So Jesus starts a religion. Or more precisely, Jesus starts a distinct community, and when the ancient world fished around for a word to describe this sort of community, as they had never seen anything like it, they settled on the world "religion." I have heard people say that Jesus did not start a religion. That's a pretty anachronistic thing to say, because it presupposes that there were things called "religions" when Jesus was around. For the pagans, there were cults to many different deities. For the monotheistic and ethnically-defined people called the Jews, there was being Jewish, which was legal, cultic, cultural, spiritual, and historical all at the same time.

But Jesus did certainly found a well-defined community: he appointed leaders for it, delegated authority to them, gave them an ethical code, a particular and novel vision of God as Father, a mission to carry out, a rite of initiation for new members, a rite of memorial to assert their identity, and he gave them a prayer to recite: "Our Father, who art in heaven . . ."[7] It may involve a personal (or communal) relationship with God, but not only did Jesus start *a* religion, he started *the first religion*. Jesus founded this community, *which was not ethnically defined*, and he sent them out to the ends of the earth to spread this good news, that one could prepare for the arrival of the Kingdom of God by repenting, and demonstrate

---

6   I would also note that in Romans 11:28–29 Paul seems to recognize a unique redemptive, eschatological role for ethnic Israel in the end times.

7   In each of these elements there are aspects of continuity with the different forms of Judaism that existed in the first century. Moreover, the Church has throughout the centuries not appreciated this continuity. In recent decades there has been a flourishing of scholarship exploring this topic, which we can summarize in the phrase "the Jewishness of Jesus." For further scholarship the reader is referred to scholars like C. E. B. Cranfield, W. D. Davies, J. D. G. Dunn, John P. Meier, Ben F. Meyer, Mark Nanos, E. P. Sanders, and N. T. Wright among others.

one's repentance by being baptized. This was entry into the Kingdom of God, which was characterized by a certain structure of power (on this, see Mary's Magnificat in Lk 1:46-55), and some very clear ethics and instructions about how to relate to God and those around you, which is the focus of the Sermon on the Mount. This movement grew, and attracted the ridicule of some of the intelligentsia, with one person scoffing at this "religion of slaves and women."[8]

Jesus had one, and only one, strategy for how this community would grow and expand to the ends of the earth: discipleship. Not seminaries, Christian schools, or evangelistic crusades—though all of these things have good components. Discipleship means teaching by modeling, sort of like an apprentice learns how to make horseshoes or like I learned how to change brakes—by watching my friend Sam do it and then trying it under his supervision. It is easy to look at the church in the USA today and wonder what went wrong—we don't have much discipleship going on. But it is there, in personal relationships as Christians learn how to be Christians (literally, *little Christs*) from their friends, their pastors, their priests, their parents and grandparents, and their neighbors. It rarely is related to a specific activity or Sunday school program, but it is there beneath the surface, only occasionally making its presence explicit. Discipleship was the method.

And the power? Jesus had an idea about this too. The old Israel was only occasionally visited by the Holy Spirit in the person of a Spirit-filled judge or prophet. But Jesus would ask his Father, and the Father would send the Spirit to remain in Jesus' Church forever. This fulfilled the prophecy from Joel, as Peter points out at Pentecost.

In conclusion: Jesus mediated a new covenant between man and God. He claimed to be both the suffering servant who would reconcile humanity to God through his death, and also the apocalyptic judge and eternal ruler of the world. Humanity would have a period of time to prepare for the final judgment, and in order to warn people of this judgment and call them to repentance, he founded a community called the Church. He gave the Church a method called discipleship, and his Father imbued it with the power of the Holy Spirit to carry out this work inviting people to

---

8   See Origen's *Contra Celsus* Book 3, Chapter 49.

repent and be baptized, so preparing themselves for the conclusion of human history and the final judgment. In doing this, Jesus founded the most successful movement in history. He did all of this in a mere three years of public ministry, and this is how he became the single most important and influential person in human history.

Discussion Questions

The author argues that Jesus founded "the first religion," but some consider Judaism to be "the first religion," and others think the word "religion" is properly understood as "private spirituality" as the secular world order would argue? Discuss.

The author argues that Jesus envisioned discipleship as Jesus' one and only strategy for extending the Kingdom of God. How can churches today have more discipleship?

What is the difference between "replacement" and "fulfillment" theology proposed by the author? Some have argued that fulfillment theology is simply a category of replacement theology. What do you think?

The author proposes a minority position—that the primary purpose of the Church is discipleship. A more common answer is that the purpose of the Church is to worship and glorify God. Compare and contrast. To what extent, if any, are these really two different answers?

Five

MUHAMMAD, THE PROPHET AND STATESMAN

The setting of Muhammad's life

But now let us turn to Islam and Muhammad, who (from a secular and historical point of view, at least) may well be the second most important and influential person ever.

With Jesus I did not attempt to give a detailed biography and with Muhammad I will likewise not do so. Rather, my purpose is to sketch the contours of his life so that we can understand how God was using Muhammad in the Islamic metanarrative in order to respond to the fundamental problem proposed by Islam—ignorance of God's will, but not the entry of death (and hence sin) in the universe.

In the Islamic story this is the context: the Jews had not been good custodians of their prophets' messages, and the Christians were in a questionable situation, worshiping Jesus, a mere prophet, along with God. This opened them to the accusation of *shirk* or association, which is a great sin in Islam. To associate something with God is to make the claim that there is something or someone who is *like* God in some essential way. This is seen as a violation of the Qur'anic teaching: "Lo! Allah pardoneth not that partners should be ascribed unto Him. He pardoneth all save that to whom He will. Whoso ascribeth partners unto Allah hath wandered far astray" (4:116).

Among the Arabs, however, most were pagans, though there were communities of Christians among them, and some Arab Jews, who had presumably converted to Judaism or were Jews who had been culturally Arabized, or both.

The story begins in Mecca, though, which did not have an indigenous, significant population of Christians or Jews. Indeed, we have only a few accounts of Muhammad ever meeting any Christians personally. This may help account for his poor understanding of basic Christian doctrines, like the Trinity, which he seems to think consists of God, Jesus, and Mary, which of course no orthodox Christian has ever believed.[1] Mecca, in any case, was pagan. It was a city on a caravan route and also received pagan pilgrims who would worship at its Ka'ba, the big black cube I mentioned above in reference to Abraham. According to the basic Islamic story,[2] Muhammad was born in 570 shortly after his father's death. His mother died when he was young and he was left in the care of a grandfather who also died, and then an uncle. He was a trader and, according to a pious Muslim tradition, illiterate, but he developed a reputation for being honest and trustworthy. He married a woman who was about 19 years older than him named Khadija who, it appears, had Christian relatives. She was wealthy and Muhammad benefitted from her wealth.

The beginning of his prophetic career

Once a year Muhammad would retreat to a cave for a time of solitude and during one of these retreats he was seized by an invisible power from behind, which terrified him, and he was told *"write!"* He responded that he did not know how to write. This happened again and he responded the

---

1   5:116

2   Dawood Translation. As with the Gospel material above, I am sticking to what Muslims believe, not what may in fact be true. For instance, there is a small but important body of scholarship that questions the actual existence of a historical figure named Muhammad. Similarly with the Jesus material above, there is a strong trend in some Christian circles to understand the Gospel of John as being very minimally based on the actual historical words of Jesus. These movements are interesting, perhaps, but they do not represent orthodoxy or reflect what Muslims and Christians actually believe, which is more important than what actually happened—if indeed there is a difference.

same way. This happened a third time, but with the command *"recite!"* And that was the beginning of the Qur'anic revelations, when surah 96:1-5 was given:

Recite in the name of the Lord who created—
created man from clots of blood
Recite! Your Lord is the Most Bountiful One,
who by the pen
taught man what he did not know.[3]

Muhammad was pretty scared by all of this and he shared the experience with his wife. She then brought a monk into the picture, a relative of hers, named Waraqa bin Nawfal. He was likely a Christian of what is today the Assyrian Church of the East and knew Syriac, and he concluded that this mysterious force was none other than the messenger angel of the Bible, Gabriel. Muhammad would, from time to time, receive verses from this angel in different ways. Here is a hadith that explains the various ways these revelations came to him from Gabriel.

Narrated 'Aisha: (the mother of the faithful believers) Al-Harith bin Hisham asked Allah's Messenger "O Allah's Messenger! How is the Divine Inspiration revealed to you?" Allah's Messenger replied, "Sometimes it is (revealed) like the ringing of a bell, this form of Inspiration is the hardest of all and then this state passes off after I have grasped what is inspired. Sometimes the Angel comes in the form of a man and talks to me and I grasp whatever he says." 'Aisha added: Verily I saw the Prophet being inspired divinely on a very cold day and noticed the sweat dropping from his forehead (as the Inspiration was over).[4]

At this point, let me talk a little about hadiths and what these are, though when we get to the part on shari'a we will learn about them in greater detail. Suffice to say that a *hadith* is a narrative of an account, event, or saying relating (usually) to the Prophet or perhaps to one of his companions.

---

3   Note how these verses show Allah responding to the ignorance of humans by *teaching* them.
4   *Al Bukhari*, volume 1, number 2.

There are various collections of hadiths made by different scholars. The majority of our information about Muhammad's life and his decisions about religious, ethical, and political matters (which is to say, the basis of the shari'a) is not from the Qur'an, but from these collections of hadiths.

We don't really have anything like this in Christianity today: imagine, though, that aside from the Bible we had several volumes of sayings and events that allegedly went back to Jesus and the Apostles.[5] Then imagine that these had become so various and multiplied, that it became necessary for scholars to evaluate carefully which ones of these were authentic (*sahiih* is the Arabic used), and that four or so collections containing only these *sahiih* events were eventually produced.[6] Then further imagine that these scholars categorized these hadiths, using headings like Fasting, Wills and Testaments, Prophets, Medicine, Dress, Tricks, Apostates, Bathing, and so on. Now imagine that each of these starts with a chain of attribution, which (allegedly) goes back to the source itself (Jesus or an Apostle). This chain of attribution is important because you can evaluate the character and trustworthiness of each person in that chain, rooting out people who were tricky or dishonest, which is to say people who may have fabricated a hadith for their own benefit (and this certainly did happen). Imagine all of this, and you will have a good idea of what is meant by *hadith*.

In these early days of his career in Mecca, Muhammad focused on issues of social justice and monotheism. He made powerful enemies–as did Jesus–because his emphasis on monotheism and not worshiping idols was antagonistic to one of the main sources of income for people in Mecca: the pagan pilgrims who came to the Ka'ba.[7] Many of the more irenic[8]

---

5   Some might say that the apocryphal gospels are for Christians like the hadith are for Muslims. The analogy is false because no normative Christian doctrine, law, or practice comes from those texts. Furthermore, aside from experts very few Christians know anything about these texts, while Muslims can often quote to you multiple hadith.

6   Other collections of hadith exist, but the compilers of those collections are not considered to have been as thorough and rigorous in ensuring that only authentic hadiths were included in their compilations. Most Muslim scholars who defend the tradition concede this.

7   An interesting parallel is the opposition faced by Paul and his companions in Ephesus in the book of Acts.

8   Irenic is (more or less) a synonym of peaceful, but I prefer to use it throughout this book because it is an antonym of polemic, whereas the antonym of peaceful is violent. Violent as an adjective has connotations of physicality, whereas the connotation of polemic is more rhetorical than physical.

and aesthetic passages from the Qur'an are from this period, though this period is not lacking in threats of hellfire for disobeying Allah and his Prophet.

Khadijah died and Muhammad married a woman named Sawda, and about a year after that was betrothed to a young girl named A'isha, daughter of one of his first converts whose actual name is unclear, but is recognized by his patronym: Father of Bakr, or Abu Bakr. A'isha was about six when they were married and about nine when Muhammad had sex with her. Here is the account in her own words:

> Narrated Aisha: The prophet engaged me when I was a girl of six. We went to Medina and stayed at the home of Harith Kharzraj. Then I got ill and my hair fell down. Later on my hair grew (again) and my mother, Um Ruman, came to me while I was playing in a swing with some of my girl friends. She called me, and I went to her, not knowing what she wanted to do to me. She caught me by the hand and made me stand at the door of the house. I was breathless then, and when my breathing became all right, she took some water and rubbed my face and head with it. Then she took me into the house. There in the house I saw some Ansari women who said, "Best wishes and Allah's blessing and a good luck." Then she entrusted me to them and they prepared me (for the marriage). Unexpectedly Allah's messenger came to me in the forenoon and my mother handed me over to him, and at that time I was a girl of nine years of age."[9]

---

9 *Al Bukhari*, volume 5, number 234. I have mostly avoided a lot of academic texts and references in this book because it is not written primarily for an academic audience. But this point makes even Muslims so uncomfortable that they often do not believe it or accept it. It is, however, incontrovertible. (For more details on why this is the case see 'A'isha' in *The Qur'an: an Encyclopedia*, Oliver Leaman ed, New York, London: Routledge, 2006.) The consummation of the marriage took place about seven months after the *hijra* or migration to Yathrib in 622. Muslims will counter that Arab girls matured very quickly in those days, and that she had her menarche (first menstrual bleeding) at the age of nine, and thus it was both ethical and permissible for him to have sex with her, and even some Christian apologists for Islam seem to buy this explanation. Even if she did in fact experience menarche at the age of nine, I cannot imagine that she would be psychologically and emotionally ready for the sexual act with a husband in his 50s.

The migration to Yathrib:
Muhammad becomes a political and military ruler

Now, to the migration (622), which is the beginning of the Islamic calendar. The city of Yathrib[10] was an oasis, and unlike Mecca it did have an indigenous, permanent Jewish population. Two of the main tribes in the city were feuding and they invited Muhammad to reside among them and settle the dispute. This is the spiritual and psychological turning point in the history of Muhammad's life and work, and thus in Islam. As I wrote earlier, Islam is the psyche of Muhammad written large. It is during this period that the texture of the Qur'anic revelations changes substantially. From being a persecuted prophet with a largely spiritual message, he is transformed into a statesman, and he competently centralized all power into his own hands—military, juridical, religious, spiritual.

Here is a section from Ali Dashti's outstanding study of the Prophet, *Twenty-three Years*[11], on the change that took place:

> After the move to Madina [an alternate spelling of Medina] at the age of 53, i.e. at an age when most men's physical and emotional faculties are on the wane, a new Mohammad emerged. During his last ten years, which he spent at Madina, he was not the same man as the Mohammad who for thirteen years had been preaching humane compassion at Mecca. The Prophet bidden by God "to warn your tribe, your nearest kin" *(sura* 26, verse 214) reappeared in the garb of the Prophet intent on subduing his own tribe and on humbling the kinsmen who for thirteen years had mocked him. Shedding the gown of the warner to "the mother town (i.e. Mecca) and the people around it" *(sura* 42, verse 5), he donned the armour of the warrior who was to bring all Arabia from the Yaman to Syria under his flag.

---

10   Yathrib today is often called Medina, which is Arabic for *city* because Yathrib became *madinat al nebi*, or the city of the Prophet.

11   Ali Dashti (1994), *23 Years: A Study of the Prophetic Career of Mohammad.* F. R. C. Bagley Translator. Dashti's hope was to produce a scholarly and critical biography of Muhammad, but his first edition had to be published outside of Iran (in Lebanon) and without his name attached to it. Likewise, Dashti had asked Bagley to translate the book (written in Farsi) into English, but only after his death. The PDF of the Bagley translation can be found online.

The beauty and melody of the Meccan *suras,* so reminiscent of the preachings of Isaiah and Jeremiah and evocative of the fervour of a visionary soul, seldom reappear in the Madinan *suras,* where the poetic and musical tone tends to be silenced and replaced by the peremptory note of rules and regulations.

At Madina orders and rules were issued on the authority of a commander who could allow no infringement or deviation. The penalties prescribed for violation or negligence were very severe. (pp 81, 82)

It appears that Muhammad originally supposed that his prophetic ministry would be welcomed by the Christians and the Jews. He referenced many of their own prophets—from Noah to Abraham to David—and affirmed monotheism with them. The Arabic word *allah* is etymologically very close to the Hebrew *el* which is often pluralized in Hebrew as *elohim.*[12] Eventually it became clear to him that this was not the case and his relationship with the other monotheistic traditions, and most especially with the Jews, began to sour. In one of the bloodiest and most problematic series of episodes in his career, Muhammad permitted and blessed the wholesale elimination of the three Jewish tribes of Yathrib, expropriating their real property, forcing their children into slavery and women into concubinage, and exiling or executing the men. Muslim apologists defend this by saying that the Jews had failed to uphold their side of a legal agreement, but this argument misses the point: even if one is legally entitled to do such a thing, can it ever be right? Whatever one's answer may be, the resulting influx of wealth, slaves, and land for the Muslims was a great boon and Muhammad's stature was confirmed.[13]

Muhammad and the shari'a

It is during this period in Yathrib that many of the basic principles of shari'a come into being. After all, while in Mecca, Muhammad did not have

---

12   It goes without saying that Allah is much closer to the Hebrew than our own English word *God* which is entirely pagan in its origins.

13   For details on the three tribes and how they were each dealt with see Ephraim Karsh, *Islamic Imperialism* (Yale University Press, 2006), chapter 1.

a growing city (and later empire) to govern. Now he did, and important questions arose. How should the spoils of war be divided? Is having sex with slave women permitted? What is the value of a woman's testimony in a court of law? When is jihad to be engaged in? How is inheritance to be divided? What is the status of slaves? How many wives may a Muslim take? How are accusations of adultery to be addressed? May interest be charged or paid?

Ali Dashti reflects on the change in tone:

> The apostle who had so movingly preached faith and compassion at Mecca gradually changed course at Madina and began to issue orders for war: "Fighting is prescribed for you" (2:212); "Fight those who do not believe. . . . !" (9:29); "If anyone desires a religion other than Islam, it will not be accepted from him" (3:79); "When you meet unbelievers, it is (a matter of) smiting necks. Then, after you have cowed them with much slaughter, fasten the bonds tight!" (47:4)
>
> Dozens of equally stern verses were revealed at Madina. The value of iron, unmentioned at Mecca, is appraised as follows in verse 25 of the Madinan sura 57: "And We sent down iron, (because) in it lie great power and benefits for the people, and so that God in the unseen world may know who support Him and His Apostles." At Mecca, so it seems, either iron had not existed or God in His omniscience had not given thought to means of identifying His and His Prophets' adversaries; for at Mecca God had commanded Mohammad to "summon (people) to your Lord's path with wisdom and good preaching, and argue with them by (using arguments) that are better! Your Lord knows well who have erred from His path, and He knows well who have been (rightly) guided" (16:126).[14]

Muhammad's animosity against the Meccans continued. After a number of battles, though, Muhammad emerged victorious, gaining permission to enter Mecca where he destroyed the idols in the Ka'ba, but then revealed that since it had been built by Abraham it should remain a center of Muslim pilgrimage. This savvy compromise meant that the income from pilgrims would not be in danger after all.

---

14   Page 74 of the online PDF version.

Muhammad was a brilliant and intelligent man. I don't think there is any way to deny that. Was he ruthless, though? Like many great political leaders, he oscillated between magnanimous generosity and violence.

Here is a hadith about God's forgiveness of a prostitute because of her simple act of kindness to a dog (an unclean animal):

> Abu Huraira reported: The Prophet, peace and blessings be upon him, said, "A prostitute saw a dog lolling around a well on a hot day and hanging his tongue from thirst. She drew some water for it in her shoe, so Allah forgave her."[15]

Here is what I think is a wise and positive hadith about justice and rulers:

> He who has been a ruler over ten people will be brought shackled on the Day of Resurrection, until the justice (by which he ruled) loosens his chains or tyranny brings him to destruction.[16]

On the other hand, we have the account of Asma bint Marwan. She was a pagan Arab poetess who ridiculed Muhammad and his verse. Provoked, Muhammad asked his men for a volunteer to assassinate her, and one complied right away.[17] We also have the story of the beautiful Jewess Safiyya bint Huyayy who, after the slaughter of her tribe, the Banu Nadir, including her father and husband, was freed from slavery and married right away to the Prophet. She was 17 and he was 62.[18]

The Qur'an and hadith hint at a lack of household stability in the Prophet's home. Over the course of his life he would have over ten wives, but never more than eight at a time—a dispensation given to him by Allah, whereas other Muslim men could only take four. His wives formed factions, competing for his attention and affection. Here is one such account:

> Narrated 'Ubaid bin 'Umar: I heard A'isha saying,

---

15 *Sahih Muslim* number 2245.
16 *Al-Tirmidhi*, Hadith1037
17 The story is related in Ibn Ishaq's *Sirat Rasul Allah* commonly called in English *The Life of the Prophet*. This is the earliest biography of the Prophet and was written by a Muslim.
18 *Sahih al Bukhari*, Hadith 522

The Prophet used to stay for a long while with Zanab bint Jahsh and drink honey at her house. So Hafsa and I decided that if the Prophet came to anyone of us, she should say [to] him, "I detect the smell of Maghafir (a nasty smelling gum) in you. Have you eaten Maghafir?' " So the Prophet visited one of them and she said to him similarly. The Prophet said, "Never mind, I have taken some honey at the house of Zainab bint Jahsh, but I shall never drink of it anymore."

So there was revealed: 'O Prophet! Why do you ban (for you) that which Allah has made lawful for you . . . If you two (wives of Prophet) turn in repentance to Allah,' (66.1-4) addressing Aisha and Hafsa. 'When the Prophet disclosed a matter in confidence to some of his wives' (66.3) namely his saying: But I have taken some honey.

Here we find Allah coming to the Prophet's defense because of the jealousy of some of his wives, and those verses whereby Allah vindicated his Prophet are in the Qur'an today.

We also find the following interesting hadith:

It is related from A'isha that the wives of the messenger of Allah fell into two parties. One party contained A'isha, Hafsa, Safiyya and Sawda, and the other party contained Umm Salama and the rest of the wives of the messenger of Allah.

The Muslims knew of the love of the messenger of Allah for A'isha, so when any of them had a gift which he wanted to give to the messenger of Allah he would delay it until the messenger of Allah was in A'isha's house. Then the person with the gift would send it to the messenger of Allah while he was in A'isha's house.

The party of Umm Salama spoke about it and said to her, "Tell the messenger of Allah to speak to the people and say, 'Whoever wants to give a gift to the messenger of Allah should give it to him in the house of whichever wife he is.'" [Muhammad refuses to speak about it with her.]

He [Muhammad] went around to her [Umm Salama] and she spoke to him. He said to her, "Do not injure me regarding A'isha. The revelation does not come to me when I am in the garment of any woman except A'isha." She said, "I repent to Allah from injuring you, Messenger of Allah."

Then they called Fatima, the daughter of the messenger of Allah, and sent her to the messenger of Allah to say, "Your wives ask you by Allah for fairness regarding the [A'isha]." [Fatima] spoke to him and he said, "O my daughter, do you not love what I love?" She said, "Yes indeed." She returned to them and informed them. They said, "Go back to him," but she refused to go back.

They sent Zaynab bint Jahsh and she went to him and spoke harshly, saying. "Your wives ask you by Allah for fairness regarding [A'isha]." She raised her voice until she turned to A'isha, who was sitting down, and abused her until the messenger of Allah looked at A'isha to see if she would speak. A'isha spoke to answer Zaynab until she had silenced her.

The prophet looked at A'isha and said, 'She is indeed the daughter of Abu Bakr.' [19]

A Muslim is only to take more than one wife if he can treat them equally. Here, a group of Muhammad's wives is upset because it is clear to everyone that he loves A'isha more than his other wives. Since the people know this, they bring him gifts when he is with her, assuming reasonably that he will be in a good mood. A group of his wives try various strategies to challenge him on this preference for A'isha. Ultimately he explains that inspiration, which is to say verses of his Qur'an, only come to him when he is dressed in A'isha's garment. This is why he loves A'isha more than his other wives—that is when the angel talks to him, when he is dressed in her garment.

I'm not so interested in the apparent cross-dressing—perhaps there is some cultural reason for this of which we're not aware. But the fact that Muhammad was not able to treat all of his wives equally. So why then did he get married to so many women? We certainly don't get the image that everyone was happy here, and at the end when Zaynab comes in to upbraid Muhammad he does not respond, and then she upbraids A'isha. A'isha then lays into Zaynab until she is quiet. At this point Muhammad commends her quick wit and shrewd response by saying that she resembles her father, Abu Bakr. From the Muslim point of view this indicates

---

19 *Sahiih al Bukhari*, Chapter 52, Number 2442. I have quoted this entire, lengthy hadith because if I summarized its content, someone would say I'm misquoting it.

the lack of faith and obedience on the part of the perfect man's wives; from the Christian (or secular, for that matter) point of view, it is a dysfunctional and unhappy family.

Muhammad and the People of the Book

The Qur'an is equivocal about the People of the Book, which is to say Jews and Christians.[20] The Christian monks earn praise with this oft-cited verse:

> Yet they are not all alike. There are among the People of the Book some upright men who all night long recite the revelations of God and worship him . . . (3:113, Dawood)

Emphasizing what Muslims have in common with the People of the Book we find this verse:

> . . . who believe in God and the Last Day; and enjoin justice and forbid evil and vie with each other in good works. They are righteous men . . . (3:114, Dawood)

The following verse seems to leave open the possibility that Jews and Christians might even enter paradise:

> Lo! Those who believe (in that which is revealed unto thee, Muhammad), and those who are Jews, and Christians, and Sabaeans - whoever believeth in Allah and the Last Day and doeth right - surely their reward is with their Lord, and there shall no fear come upon them neither shall they grieve. (2:62, Pickthall)

Moreover, food prepared by Jews or Christians is thus made *hallal*[21] (though pork is never *hallal*):

---

20 Though later in history Muslim scholars would include other non-Muslim religious communities, like Zoroastrians, under this heading.

21 That is, permitted according to the shari'a; as opposed to *haram* or forbidden things.

This day are (all) good things made lawful for you. The food of those who have received the Scripture is lawful for you, and your food is lawful for them. (5:5, Pickthall)

There is also the implication, though, that most of the Jews and Christians who heard Muhammad were not rightly guided. Because of this, there is expectation that *authentic* Jews and Christians would recognize the validity of Muhammad's message and believe in it. Which is to say, they would become Muslims:

And when it is recited to them, they say: "We believe therein, for it is the Truth from our Lord: indeed we have been Muslims (bowing to Allah's Will) from before this." (28:53, Yusuf Ali)

Some of the Jews changed the Scripture (or the reading thereof) they were given: "But the transgressors changed the word from that which had been given them" (2:59).

By the end of his life, it is clear that Muhammad had great enmity towards Jews and Christians, as this hadith indicates:

A'isha and Abdullah reported: As the Messenger of Allah (may peace be upon him) was about to breathe his last, he drew his sheet upon his face and when he felt uneasy, he uncovered his face and said in that very state: "Let there be curse upon the Jews and the Christians that they have taken the graves of their apostles as places of worship." He in fact warned (his men) against what they (the Jews and the Christians) did.[22]

Furthermore, we have what appears to be clear affirmation from Allah that the Torah and Gospel are to be read and applied, which logically would preclude the possibility that the texts (as opposed to how they were read) are corrupted:

How come they (come) unto thee (Muhammad) for judgment when they have the Torah, wherein Allah hath delivered judgment (for

---

22   *Sahiih Muslim*, Book 4, Number 1082

them)? . . . Lo! We did reveal the Torah, wherein is guidance and a light . . . And We caused Jesus, son of Mary, to follow in their footsteps, confirming that which was (revealed) before him in the Torah, and We bestowed on him the Gospel wherein is guidance and a light, confirming that which was (revealed) before it in the Torah - a guidance and an admonition unto those who ward off (evil). Let the People of the Gospel judge by that which Allah hath revealed therein. Whoso judgeth not by that which Allah hath revealed: such are evil-livers.

And unto thee (Muslims) have We revealed the Scripture (the Qur'an) with the truth, confirming whatever Scripture was before it, and a watcher over it. So judge between them by that which Allah hath revealed, and follow not their desires away from the truth which hath come unto thee. For each We have appointed a divine law and a traced-out way. Had Allah willed He could have made you one community. But that He may try you by that which He hath given you (He hath made you as ye are). So vie one with another in good works. Unto Allah ye will all return, and He will then inform you of that wherein ye differ. (5:43-48, Pickthall)

All in all, then, the Qur'an is equivocal regarding the status of the validity of the religion of the Jews and Christians. Some verses seem to indicate that if they live according to their religion with devotion and sincerity they will inherit paradise and their books have integrity (though some of their scholars may misinterpret those books). Other verses imply that their prophets taught Islam, and that any genuine Jew or Christian would recognize the validity of Muhammad's message and submit to it. Only recalcitrant and stubborn Jews and Christians would continue to act as if they were worshiping God while not in reality submitting to him.

Islamic tradition resolved this enigma by making the People of the Book clearly inferior to Muslims, while also recognizing that they were not atheists or pagans. As a result, unlike atheists or pagans, they could continue to live in the land of Islam, but unlike Muslims, they would have the status of second-class citizens. The clearest such gesture from the Qur'an is the *jizya*—a special tax paid by the People of the Book, which should be done in public in order to demonstrate to the entire society that they are inferior to Muslims:

Fight those who believe not in Allah nor the Last Day, nor hold that forbidden which hath been forbidden by Allah and His Messenger, nor acknowledge the religion of Truth, (even if they are) of the People of the Book, until they pay the Jizya with willing submission, and feel themselves subdued. (9:29, Yusuf Ali)

The name of the communities of the People of the Book (often misunderstood as if it were somehow a term of endearment) was *dhimmi*. *Dhimmis* are often thought to be religious minorities. This is an incorrect interpretation. The status of *dhimmi* is solely related to Muslim rule. That is all—it has nothing to do with being a minority. Indeed, there have been examples of places where 80% of the population was Christian, but because they were under Muslim rule, they were *dhimmi*.[23] We will learn more about this aspect of the shari'a in a coming chapter. For now, I want to reiterate that regarding the People of the Book Muhammad was ambivalent—wavering between being mildly positive and violently antagonistic. Since Islam is the psyche of Muhammad written large, this ambivalence has lived itself out in the wavering fortunes and often precarious status of Jews and Christians under Muslim rule throughout the centuries.

If Muhammad's family life was perhaps not ideal, he was successful in the expansion of his community. As Kenneth Cragg once said, "Muhammad, in expanding his empire, managed to start a religion." This is a great quote because it unveils the jejune classification of Islam as simply a religion. It is much more than a religion because the category itself, as we use it today, was historically construed to refer to Christianity. Islam is not the same sort of thing as Christianity; it does not belong to the same category of ways of life. Ayatolla Khomeini put it this way: "Islam is politics or it is nothing."[24]

Muhammad's vision and community

Islam, let us remember, is not responding to the same crisis that Christianity is. In the metanarrative of Islam, the failure up to this point has been

---

23   I am thinking of Anatolia under Turkish rule, mentioned in Bat Ye'or's 1996 book, *The Decline of Eastern Christianity under Islam.*

24   Quoted in Bernard Lewis' 2004 book, *From Babel to Dragomans*, p 303.

that the people entrusted with the message from God about how to act and live (Jews and Christians) have failed to preserve it well, live according to it, and make it known to all the earth. God has now responded to this in a robust and final manner: he has sent into the world the seal of the Prophets—Muhammad. Once a document is sealed, it can no longer be changed. Essentially, a seal demonstrates clearly the origin or ownership of a document.[25]

Furthermore, the structures of the Christians and the Jews had failed in their universal mission. And so Muhammad has founded a new community that is both a state and a "religion" at the same time. Cragg's use of the word *empire* to refer to the *umma* is astute, for an empire is that sort of polity wherein law is created by the command of a single person— *imperare* being the Latin word for "command," itself being related to our English word "imperative."

This *umma* spread the divine commands around the world: indeed this is its very purpose:

> Ye are the best of peoples, evolved for mankind, enjoining what is right, forbidding what is wrong, and believing in Allah. If only the People of the Book had faith, it were best for them: among them are some who have faith, but most of them are perverted transgressors. (3:110, Yusuf Ali)

Carrying out this mission of spreading and enforcing the shari'a (enjoining the right, forbidding the wrong) can be done by various avenues. This might be accomplished by military conquest, which is historically how Islam initially grew throughout the Middle East and North Africa, or it could be by inviting people to embrace Islam and informing them of the financial and societal benefits of conversion, as was the case in parts of East Africa and Indonesia and is the case today in thousands of prisons and universities throughout North America and Europe.

This *umma*, moreover, would not be ruled by the haphazard laws created by human beings, but by a detailed and meticulous body of divine

---

25   It is worth noting here that in Christianity, the sacrament of Confirmation is understood as a seal, whereby God's ownership of the confirmand is publicly and ritually demonstrated and affirmed.

laws that would touch on and provide guidance regarding every facet of life, from the smallest to the greatest detail. In the days of Muhammad the *umma* was ruled by the Prophet, and following would come his successors, the Arabic word being *xulafa'*, the singular being *xaliifa* or as the traditional transliteration into English goes, *caliph*.

Meanwhile, the government of the Christian community was entrusted to the Apostles, and as they became aware that the return of Messiah might be prolonged, they appointed other men to continue their ministries. They symbolized this by laying their hands on the heads of the men they were offering to God and his Church, the same gesture used by individuals offering animal sacrifices in the Old Testament.[26]

In these two metanarratives, then, God appoints a sort of ultimate representative, who forms a specific community. In Christianity this is called the Church, and in Islam it is called the *umma*. These two communities have their own missions. For the Church, it is to preach the Good News to the ends of the earth (precisely what the Qur'an rightly complains they did not do), baptizing new members, and then teaching them the way of Jesus—all of this together is called discipleship. For the *umma* it is to live according to God's eternal and unchanging shari'a, and with patience and wisdom, whether through war or preaching or migration, to see this spread to the last corners of the earth. The Church is responding to the entry of death into the universe, preparing it for the day when the city of God shall be with men (Rev 21) and everything will be made new. The *umma* is responding to the very real problem that humans do not know or will refuse to obey God's benevolent and unchanging will for human conduct, both personal and communal. Now let us turn in greater detail to living life within these two communities.

Discussion Questions

The author mentions the reality of the Prophet having sex with his child bride. Some Christians argue that this is a major problem in the Islamic vision of Muhammad being the ideal or perfect man. Discuss.

---

26 See for instance Leviticus 8:14.

Six

LIFE IN THE COMMUNITY

If my treatment of Jesus and Muhammad were somewhat broad, then this section will be all the more so. And it must be so. Islam and Christianity are now both over a millennium old, and have taken root in every continent, and arguably have become the two most powerful forces in the world—more than capitalism, nationalism, the scientific revolution, atheism, Communism, materialism, commercialism, any country, nation, or multinational corporation. If this doesn't seem correct to you, then ask yourself what will be around longer? Christianity and Islam have already lived through the rise and fall of empires, world wars, plagues, famines, natural disasters, economic hardships, and even the deaths of each tradition's inaugural figure–every type of biblical disaster one could imagine. Christianity and Islam will be around long after Western Civilization is dead and gone (and it is presently in a state of rapid and irreversible decline, I believe). So while a given force may rise up, it will probably not have the staying power of either of these two great movements/communities.

But what does it look like to live according to the life of these communities? I will handle these questions under three rubrics: ethics; doctrine; and ritual. It is impossible and probably undesirable to essentialize Islam and Christianity. And so, painting with broad strokes is necessary. I am confident, though, that my depictions will work for the Baptist in Texas or the Catholic in the Philippines or the Orthodox believer in Ethiopia, as well as the Shi'a in Iran, the Sunni in Guyana, and the Salafist in London.

Before beginning, I do want to clarify that I am working from a relatively conservative point of view. I learned very quickly while studying for my master of arts in theology that if something isn't at least 500 years old, it's probably little more than a fad. Often the newest, most "progressive" and modern ideas are the ones that get so much attention and show so much promise, but almost without fail are a flash in the pan. From this point of view, I think we can say that we are now coming to a point where we can make an honest assessment of those chaotic movements in Western Europe of the 16th Century which have been given the self-aggrandizing, euro-centric, and totalizing title of the Reformation. The traditional and the conservative generally indicate growing numbers. The most progressive churches in the world (including my own Episcopal Church of the USA) are not, on the whole, growing. Rather, around the whole world, the churches that are growing tend to be the most conservative and traditional ones—churches that place a great deal of importance on membership, giving, accountability, sharing your faith with those around you, and personal devotions at home or work. The same is true for Judaism. The same is also true for Islam—it is the conservative forces that are growing and becoming more powerful, not less. This is my justification for opting for a conservative summary of life in the two communities of these two metanarratives.

Ethics

Ethics is the study of right and wrong. It is a branch of philosophy and is generally heavily influenced by what one believes about God. Indeed, a key challenge to atheists is to propose a logical, objective, and non-self-refuting theory of ethics that does not collapse into relativism or subjectivism. I used to think this was possible (for the atheist) when I was studying for my bachelor of arts in philosophy, but have since changed my mind—a topic for a different book.

In Christianity, ethics flows from the eternal law, which is to say the will and being of God. God not only says this or that is good, but he himself is goodness, he is love, and he is beauty. There is a theory that says that anything that God commands is good—this is called divine command theory (DCT). I think that is what we find more or less in Islam, and we'll return to that in a moment. This is *not* what we learn from Christian ethics (though yes, there are some Christians who hold to DCT). The greater tradition of Christian ethics run from Aristotle through to Thomas Aquinas, the Italian monk who proposed a brilliant and (to me) compelling synthesis of Aristotle, the Bible, and St Augustine.[1]

Aristotle was not only a philosopher but a botanist and zoologist. He was intensely interested in learning from how nature functioned. He taught that there are different ways of answering the question, *What is it?* One is to address the material cause: it is a thing made of wood. Another is to address the formal cause: it is a thing with four legs, a square piece of wood horizontal to the floor, and another piece of wood that is perpendicular to the floor and attached on one edge to other pieces of wood. The efficient cause: it is a thing made by Joseph the carpenter. And the final cause: it is a thing to be sat on. Identifying the four causes for a thing will give you a relatively precise idea of what it is: a chair. It is this framework of thought that leads to his moral theology.

The word "virtue" is derived from the Latin word *vir*, which means *man*. The idea is that what makes a male into a man is not his age or education or earning power, but his morals—that he possesses certain qualities. Aquinas borrowed four cardinal virtues from the pre-Christian philosophers (Plato goes into these a great deal in his *Republic*), which are courage (sometimes called fortitude), temperance (sometimes called moderation), prudence, and justice. Then he also borrows three more "theological" virtues from St Paul: faith, hope, and charity.[2] There are other virtues, like honesty and religion and civility, but these are all variations or types of these seven virtues.

I teach these virtues to my kids (ages 4, 7 and 10). When they do something bad, I often ask, "Which virtue did you miss?" This means my three kids know more ethics than 99% of Americans. You will notice that *being nice* is not a virtue. Here is how I explain the virtues to them:

Courage is when you *do* the right thing even if you don't want to (maybe you're afraid, but it could be another reason).

---

1   It is not widely known, but I will mention here that Aquinas' work *summa contra gentiles* was composed in order to aid his fellow Dominicans in evangelizing Muslims in then-Muslim-ruled Spain.

2   1 Cor 13:13

Moderation is when you *don't* do something you want to, because you know it isn't right, or good for you.

Prudence is doing the right thing at the right time.

Justice is rewarding good and punishing evil (or *rendering unto each his due*, if you are feeling fancy).

So what is religion? Aquinas says it is a form of justice (and I think this is beautiful) whereby we try to render unto God what he is due. We know this is impossible, but we do it through our ministry and worship and God, in his generosity to us, accepts this.[3] Or, to be more precise, it is to participate in the Son's perfect worship of the Father by the Spirit. That is why the Father accepts our worship, because it is fused into the Son's ongoing worship as our great High Priest.

I assume that Christian readers already know about faith, hope, and love and so there should be no need to discuss them. Rather, the point here is that Christianity proposes a coherent ethical system, but tends to stay away from rules. I mean, there are rules like the Ten Commandments. But mostly there are good habits (virtues) that will help us to do the right thing no matter what the context—Palestine in the 1st Century, or China in the 7th Century, or Saudi Arabia today (yes, there are converts today even in Mecca). In sum, one has four cardinal virtues, and three theological virtues, and from these virtues, which are good moral habits, the rest of ethics flows naturally. This ethical framework is commonly called natural law ethics or virtue ethics.

Furthermore, according to Christian ethics, evil does not exist; or rather, evil does not possess its own existence, without leaching on the Good. That is to say, evil is a lack of good. Saint Augustine explains this reality thus:

> And in the universe, even that which is called evil, when it is regulated and put in its own place, only enhances our admiration of the good; for we enjoy and value the good more when we compare it with the evil. For the Almighty God, who, as even the heathen acknowledge, has supreme power over all things, being Himself supremely good, would never permit the existence of anything evil among His works,

---

3   See his *ST* II-II q.81 a.4c.; II-II q.81 a.5 and q.95 a.2 obj.2. For more on Aquinas' vision of religion as a virtue see Robert Jared Staudt's 2008 essay "Religion as Virtue" (http://www.scotthahn.com/download/attachment/3734, accessed 22 Feb 2015).

if He were not so omnipotent and good that He can bring good even out of evil. For what is that which we call evil but the absence of good? In the bodies of animals, disease and wounds mean nothing but the absence of health; for when a cure is effected, that does not mean that the evils which were present—namely, the diseases and wounds—go away from the body and dwell elsewhere: they altogether cease to exist; for the wound or disease is not a substance, but a defect in the fleshly substance,—the flesh itself being a substance, and therefore something good, of which those evils—that is, privations of the good which we call health—are accidents. Just in the same way, what are called vices in the soul are nothing but privations of natural good. And when they are cured, they are not transferred elsewhere: when they cease to exist in the healthy soul, they cannot exist anywhere else.[4]

A lie is saying something lacking truth, being greedy is lacking generosity, being a glutton or drunkard is lacking temperance, and so on. All of this stems from death (remember Genesis 3), which is a lack of life. God, being aware of this drastic problem, in the New Covenant actually sends his Spirit to dwell within us, transforming us from the inside out, so that we can bear the fruit of the Spirit, which is so clearly related to the virtues we just discussed:

> But the fruit of the Spirit is love, joy, peace, patience, kindness, good-ness, faithfulness, gentleness, self-control; against such things there is no law. And those who belong to Christ Jesus have crucified the flesh with its passions and desires.(Galatians 5:22-24)

A common complaint my Muslim friends have made to me is: you (Christians/Christianity) are the religion of love, you get to do anything you want. By this they do not mean that we get to be immoral, but that each Christian has a great deal of freedom in figuring out what the virtuous life looks like.

From the Muslim point of view this is all very fuzzy on another count too: what polity is the one designated by the Christian ethics? This ethical

---

4   St Augustine, *Enchiridion* 11, "What is Called Evil in the Universe is But the Absence of God". http://biblehub.com/library/augustine/the_enchiridion/chapter_11_what_is_called_evil.htm

framework, whether we call it virtue ethics or Natural Law ethics, does not dictate a particular form of government. Of any polity, it will indeed ask, is this a virtuous state in terms of justice? Is this a virtuous state in terms of charity? Is this a state that permits people to act according to their final cause or *telos*, which is to love God and enjoy him forever (which is to say, does it have religious freedom)? Are the expenses of this state in line with its income (temperance), or does this state continuously consume more than it produces (gluttony, which is a lack of temperance)? But the community called the Church can flourish or die in a democracy, a republic, a monarchy, an empire, a confederacy, a city-state, or a tribal government.[5] Indeed, it has flourished in each of these and many others since its beginnings. It is not wed to any particular polity though at any given point in history it tends to endorse those that allow for the flourishing of the human being to reach its *telos*.

This makes the Church fundamentally *unlike* the *umma*, which always and everywhere must be a polity, or at least in the case that there is no caliph, aspire to be a polity. This is one of the reasons for the great success of the Islamic State with its Caliph (unrecognized though he is by most Muslims). Reform groups like Al Qaeda and the Muslim Brotherhood talked about reviving the Caliphate (defunct since the 1920s with the Ottoman Empire) for decades, but the Islamic State actually *did it*. It is important to understand how, for some Muslims, this is intensely inspiring, dramatic, and encouraging—the Prophet once again has a Caliph! No wonder, then, that hundreds, maybe thousands, of youth from the USA, Canada, the UK, Germany, France, Belgium, and the Netherlands have gone to join his ranks. Just imagine what it would be like if there were no Bishop of Rome (that is, the Pope) for 90 years, and then someone finally broke through whatever logjam there was and the starved cardinals in the Sistine Chapel elected him! That would be exciting for Catholics around the world. And if he issued a call for a new religious order to the young Catholics of the world they would come in substantial numbers, I suspect.

On to Islam. That which is good is what God says is good. There are indeed virtues in Islam as in Christianity, but there is a great deal of instruc-

---

5   For what it's worth, Plato disliked democracies because he said that the population of these states tended to lack moderation. That strikes me as right on when I look at the USA today.

tion regarding how to live out those virtues. Those details are outlined in the shari'a, which is eternal, divine, and immutable. This shari'a is made known to us in two sources: 1) the Qur'an; and 2) the life of the Prophet. We know about the life of the Prophet mostly from the hadith, though the actual revelatory content is not the hadith, but the life of the Prophet which it describes; the hadith simply relates events from the life of the Prophet.[6]

The name of the process whereby humans interpret, codify, and apply this eternal, immutable shari'a is called *usul al fiqh*, which can be translated as *the derivation of Islamic jurisprudence*. In Islam this is generally considered to be the highest of all pursuits, more so than Islamic philosophy or theology.[7] The shari'a is divine, but *fiqh* is a human endeavor, and so a number of prominent schools have arisen over the centuries. When there is unanimity among them (called *ijma'*), the matter is considered as settled and cannot be revisited. *Ijma'* is a sign that the *umma* has correctly understood the eternal and immutable shari'a, which cannot be changed by human will any more than we can update the laws of planetary motion.

There is a further question: how does one identify from the texts of the Qur'an and the hadith what the shari'a, in fact, is? That is, from these two sources what methods and principles can one employ to discern the mind of God, which is to say the shari'a? There are two primary principles that can help in this: *abrogation* and *analogy*.[8]

Let us begin with abrogation.[9] The principle that later verses in the Qur'an must *abrogate* earlier verses in the Qur'an is an important principle of interpretation, or hermeneutics, because as we saw above regarding the People of the Book, the Qur'an is often ambivalent or even, apparently, contradictory. When one has two verses that appear to command things that are mutually exclusive, how does one decide which verse to follow? The answer is simple: the latter verse abrogates the earlier one. Thus, it is

---

6   It is for this reason that one often hears that the Qur'an and the hadith are the two sources for shari'a, but my explanation is more precise.

7   These two disciplines do still exist, though since the Middle Ages they have fallen on hard times.

8   I am aware of other methods for the derivation of Islamic jurisprudence like *maslaha*, *istihsaan, istislaah*, and so on. While these are interesting and important for a comprehensive understanding of how *fiqh* has been carried out at certain points in time and in certain places, here I am only aiming at a basic introduction to the topic, and not all scholars agree that these methods were or are legitimate.

9   In Arabic this is called *nasx wa mansuux*

the verses that came to Muhammad later in his life that are the operative and controlling ones. These verses are, by and large, the ones most focused on Jihad and warfare—an uncomfortable truth.

A classic example of this is the progressive revelation regarding alcohol.[10] At first alcohol was permitted, then a warning against alcohol was issued confirming that it may benefit people but there is also danger in it, and then finally alcohol was forbidden entirely. The principle of abrogation is clearly enunciated in the Qur'an with the following verse:

> If We abrogate a verse or cause it to be forgotten, We will replace it by a better one or one similar. Did you not know that God has power over all things? (2:106, Dawood)

The explanation given for this concept is that God knew that humans, in their ignorance and fragility, were not able to assimilate the complete and correct vision of Islam and its ordered, ethical life (the shari'a), and so God, in his kindness to us, *gradually* revealed the fullness of his truth. Abrogation functions both within the Qur'an (as in the example above), but it also applies to previous revelations. For instance, one night I was with some Muslim friends and we were discussing whether it was okay to follow Jesus' lead and call God "our Father." One of them responded that it was okay at the time of Jesus and up until the time of Muhammad. The implication was clear: that God had permitted humans to address him with this intimate term, Father, but that after the final prophet came the issue had to be cleared up, and since Muhammad never did this, neither should we. Or with the dietary rules of the Torah: the Torah was correct about forbidding pork, but its teachings on shellfish were abrogated, because everything from the sea is *hallal* (which is to say, permitted, or kosher).[11] All in all, this hermeneutical tool of abrogation helps us to determine which verse is authoritative—whichever one came later.

There is also the use of analogy or *qiyas*. In logic, an analogy is the process of arguing from similarity in known respects to similarity in un-

---

10　Incidentally, the word *alcohol* is an Arabic word (note the definite article *al* at the beginning of the word).

11　Another way to address this issue would be for the Muslim to say that the text of the Torah originally had the correct information, but that it was later corrupted.

known respects. In *fiqh*, analogy takes events from the life of the Prophet in the 7th Century and problems from other places and periods of history and tries to relate them in order to discern how God's shari'a applies to them. Consider the example of alcohol. The Qur'an only explicitly forbids a few types of local fermented drinks they had in Arabia at the time. It says nothing about tequila, vodka, or rice wine (sake). But we know that wine is similar to these other things, for they all can cause drunkenness when consumed in excess. And so, all fermented drinks are forbidden.

Analogy was also at the heart of Osama bin Laden's explanation as to why the 9/11 attacks were legitimate acts of self-defense. America was actively persecuting Muslims around the world. It supported Israel which had allegedly taken away the homes and lands of Muslims in Palestine, it profaned Arabia by having military forces there, and so on. We read in one of the late chapters of the Qur'an the following verse:

> Leave is given to those who fight because they were wronged—surely God is able to help them who were expelled from their habitations without right, except that they say "Our Lord is God." Had God not driven back the people, some by the means of others, there had been destroyed cloisters and churches, oratories and mosques, wherein God's Name is much mentioned. Assuredly God will help him who helps Him—surely God is All-strong, All-mighty. (22:39–40, Arberry)

Al Qaeda, in the 9/11 attacks, understood itself to be operating under this principle.[12] They viewed the pagans chasing the Muslims out of Mecca (which is what Muhammad was referring to in that verse) as analogous to America employing its commercial and economic might to persecute Muslims, whether directly or indirectly. There are many other verses we could draw on to show why Al Qaeda's claim to being an authentic practice of Islam is not unreasonable, but our purpose is here is to explain the principle of analogy as a tool for applying the divine and perfect shari'a to practical situations that arise today.

What about decapitations and crucifixions, like those practiced by the

---

12   Osama bin Laden's "Letter to America" can be found translated into English at
     www.theguardian.com/world/2002/nov/24/theobserver, accessed 7 Jan 2015.

Islamic State? It is an error to dismiss these acts as "un-Islamic." Western-
ers often exclude from their interpretation of Islam things they don't agree
with. It is a misunderstanding of Islamic goals and aims, and some might
regard this willful ignorance as an insult to thousands of men and women
who are genuinely enthused by the revival of the Caliphate. Some of them
have left safety and security in North America and Europe to go and "fight
in the way of Allah." I also find it offensive that just because their use of violence is not easily comprehensible to the narrow and shallow Western mind
that we dismiss their piety and devotion as nothing more than "radicalism"
or "terrorism" or "not Islam." As a Christian, I do not believe what they are
doing is ethical or that it glorifies God, but to claim they are mere "thugs"
who don't know anything about Islam is patently false. One of the latest
surahs in the Qur'an is *The Spoils* or *Al Anfaal*. The name comes from the
fact that in this surah Allah gives specific instructions about how to divide
the booty of jihad, and it is here that we find one of the verses on beheading:

> When your Lord revealed to the angels: I am with you, therefore make
> firm those who believe. I will cast terror into the hearts of those who
> disbelieve. Therefore strike off their heads and strike off every fingertip
> of them. (8:12, Shakir)

A few points: First, this is a late verse and is not abrogated by any other
verse (Though of course it may abrogate earlier irenic verses). Second, the
Arabic is unequivocal here. Third, there can be no question as to whether
decapitation is permitted or not; indeed, it is mandated. Under certain circumstances God *commands* decapitation quite clearly. The only question
is: *when?* What is the proper analogy between the situation of Muhammad
and our situation today? One might answer that Jews and Christians are
People of the Book, while the Meccans were pagans, meaning there can be
no analogy. Another response would be that Muhammad was engaging in
self-defense, but as we have seen above, when you believe everyone is out
to get you then most any act can be construed as self-defense. My point
is that we should understand that there are good reasons why Muslims
would be able to look at the decapitations of the Islamic State and say they
are not according to the shari'a, because there is not a proper analogy between Muhammad's context and the situation of the Islamic State today.

On the other hand, when people say that they *are* in accord with shari'a, we cannot dismiss the possibility out of hand. Muhammad was told to utilize decapitation against those who opposed him and the growth of the *umma*, and this is what the Islamic State is doing today.

In summary, the shari'a is revealed to us in two different sources: the Qur'an, and the *sunna* or life of Muhammad. The hermeneutic of abrogation helps us select the authoritative portion of the Qur'an or hadith when there is an apparent contradiction. And then there are two primary principles or methods that help us to derive that shari'a: analogy and consensus (*ijma'*, which was addressed above).

The action of independent legal reasoning (rather than simply citing an existing precedent) is called *ijtihaad*. There is debate about who is able to engage in this activity, and whether or not this process was brought to a close in the 11th or 12th Centuries. A period of four or five hundred years to bring that enormous project to its closure seems pretty reasonable. However, the idea of having largely comprehended and codified the shari'a is one that is unattractive to some people in the West. They ask, why can't Muslims revise it or update it? Why can't they modernize it? Why not bring it up to date with the ideals of human rights and liberal democracy? But the whole point is to have a law that need not be updated or revised! It is a law from God! And one must ask, if the *umma* has not been able to significantly codify the shari'a by now, with over a millennium for the project, then what good is such a project? Is it even possible? Is it just chasing the wind?

In Islamic ethics, then, some things are forbidden or *haram* (pork, alcohol), other things are permitted or *hallal* (having sex with your slaves, seafood). There are still other categories, like things not forbidden but discouraged (smoking), things that have no moral bearing either way, and things that are unknown.

So Islamic ethics and Christian ethics both have a sense of qualities that should be fostered in the individual and the community, but Islam's shari'a provides a much more detailed picture of what that ethical life looks like—from how to drink a cup of water to what to say when you enter the bathroom. Of course not all Muslims keep all these rules, and many of them don't even know these rules, just as not all Christians keep or even know the rules or ethical framework of Christianity. But they all know *some* of these rules. Also, even when people don't know the rules or doctrines of their religion, it doesn't mean that they are somehow negligible or unimportant. It may be true that American Catholics don't, by and large, eschew artificial birth control as their Church says they should, but that doesn't detract from the importance of the Church's radically counter-cultural view on the matter.

The ethical systems in both metanarratives are different because they are responding to two different problems. Islam proposes that humans are good but need to know the will of God for ordering life and society: the shari'a answers precisely that need. Christians are supposed to live this life in order to attract other people to the community of the New Covenant, the Church. Also, because our community belongs to a kingdom not of this world, we should not act like this world. So we bless those who curse us, turn the other cheek, and engage in religious devotion for the sake of God. We are his coworkers in the grand project of saving the world. Finally, we live moral lives because sin is a symptom of death, and our whole mission is to live and preach the Gospel of Life, inviting all nations to repent and be baptized, and so to prepare themselves for the ineffable summation of human history—the final judgment.

Doctrines in Christianity

I don't want to focus too much on doctrine. Western civilization has tended to focus a great deal on intellectual content, as if Christianity and Islam were primarily "sets of beliefs." That is a rather wan vision of what the two metanarratives propose. They are movements; they are ways of life. I have intentionally tried to focus on the metanarrative or big story proposed by each of these movements, rather than listing their "beliefs," for this is the most fruitful and valuable approach. Nonetheless, totally passing over the beliefs that animate and are integral to the two metanarratives is impossible. The beliefs themselves grow out of the soil of these narratives.

For both Christianity and Islam, I have selected three key doctrines for consideration.

For Christianity, the three doctrines we will focus on are atonement, incarnation, and Trinity.

Atonement is a word that means, more or less, covering. In Hebrew, it is *kipur* as in Yom Kipur, the Day of Atonement, and the Arabic is a cognate: *kafaara*. The effect of the doctrine of atonement is summarized in the Nicene Creed when it says *we believe in the forgiveness of sins*. This conviction is present throughout the New Testament and became part of the ancient liturgy of the Church: *agnus dei, qui tollis pecata mundi . . .* ("Lamb of God, you take away the sins of the world"). Christianity, in recognizing the profundity of the death that has entered the universe, acknowledges that humans cannot atone for their own sins or be good enough for God. God in his love provided Jesus, a pure and unblemished sacrifice on our behalf. The result is the forgiveness of sins.

Incarnation is the logical prerequisite to atonement. According to St Anselm, a debt of honor is owed to God.[13] Humans must pay this, for we all together, as a family, have dishonored him. God's honor is infinite and so an offering of infinite value is required. God in his love provides the God-Man. Jesus Christ was one human being, completely like God in his divinity, and completely like us in his humanity, but without sin (Hebrews 4:15).[14] Therefore, he was the "one mediator between God and men, the man Christ Jesus," (1 Timothy 2:5). The doctrine of incarnation attempts to make sense of Jesus, what he said about himself, his relation to his Father, and the early Church's experience (and worship) of him.

Trinity is God's revelation to humanity regarding his own experience of who he and what he is. Specifically, that God experiences himself in three modes called Father, Son, and Holy Spirit. These are God's eternal modes of self-knowledge. The typically used words 'three persons' are somewhat misleading because the Latin word *personae* and the English word *persons* do not (today) mean the same thing. The relation of the Son to the Father is eternal generation and he is 'eternally begotten of the Father' and the man Jesus is 'the image of the invisible God' (Colossians 1:15). The name of the relationship between the Father and Spirit is procession, and in this procession and in this act of being he is thus the 'giver

---

13   I am following St Anselm's *cur deus homo* here. Some people think that Anselm taught penal substitution. This is wrong, though, as he explicitly denies the concept. Rather, he proposed a substitution of honor, as summarized very briefly here.

14   See also the *Definition of Chalcedon* of 451.

of life.' The word *procession* is a technical, theological word, and comes from John 15:26: '. . . the Spirit of truth, who proceeds from the Father. . . .'

The quality of the Father is that he is uncreated and the fountainhead of all being, divinity, and existence. The indivisible essence of God as he experiences himself is revealed to us as love, holiness, and beauty, which in turn are all refractions of *being*.

Doctrines in Islam

For Islam, the three doctrines I will highlight are: Muhammad as Seal of the Prophets; the Increate Nature of the Qur'an; and Monadic Monotheism.[15]

Muhammad as Seal of the Prophets: This doctrine is important for at least two reasons. One, it means there is a finality to what God is revealing and thus a beginning can be made in discerning his divine law (the shari'a). This means there is an end to abrogation. What we have in the Qur'an is final and there is no other information or material to reveal. Two, on a practical level it means that no legitimate religions can be founded after Islam—not Baha'ism, not Mormonism, not Ahmadi Islam, not Scientology. This may seem like an esoteric point, but it means that Baha'is living in Egypt and Iran cannot have their religions recognized officially.

The Increate[16] Nature of the Qur'an: In the early days of Islam there was a significant and important controversy about the nature of the Qur'an. One party, known as the mu'tazila were rationalistic in their theory and proposed that the Qur'an was a created thing, and could thus be examined critically like other books. They lost the battle to a group called the Ash'arites who argued that the Qur'an is increate with God, while not being the same thing as God. This poses a difficulty because it looks like the sin of *shirk* or association—for what is eternal but God alone? This eternality of the Qur'an supports my statement that the Qur'an is more like Jesus (the final and complete revelation of God's eternal Word) than

---

15 See *tawhiid* in the glossary.
16 That is, having the status of existing but never having been created; eternality.

the Bible. It also should help people understand why the issue of how the Qur'an as a physical book is treated is so sensitive to some Muslims.

For instance, Muslims never place the Qur'an on a chair or seat or the floor. Rather it is usually put on the highest shelf to demonstrate its exalted nature. The common practice of some Christians of writing notes in the margins of the Bible is unthinkable to Muslims, because it is seen as treating the divine book as little more than a notepad.

Monadic Monotheism: As opposed to Trinitarian monotheism (Christianity), Islam proposes that God is a monad. In reference to us it is clear that Lordship over the universe belongs to him alone, and our worship must be only to him and no others (that would be *shirk*). While we cannot name the essence of God, we can name some characteristics or "names" that describe his actions or dispositions at a given time: thus he may be the one who guides rightly and the one who leads astray simultaneously to different people; he may be "truth" and the "schemer" simultaneously to different people. The Qur'an teaches that "there is nothing like unto Him" (42:11) and so we should be content with using these divine names or attributes, but without asking how precisely they are true.[17]

At this point we find something surprising in our metanarratives: in each, the difference in the nature of the one God—Trinitarian vs. Monadic—results in a different vision of the human being—which is to say theological anthropology. This is the basic point of departure in our metanarratives. A monadic God cannot experience love or be loving within himself, for the very nature of love is to sacrifice one's own good for another. *Apart from creation and creatures to love, the deity of Islam can neither essentially be loved nor love*[18]. This is why we have two different answers regarding the final cause (*telos*) of man: in Christianity it is to love God and enjoy him

---

17 See 'Tawhid' in *The Qur'an: An Encyclopedia*, Oliver Leaman ed. (2005) for more details on this complex issue.

18 I have included the word "essentially" here intentionally. There are traditions within Sufi Islam where there is a focus on experiencing the being of God himself and this is sometimes spoken of in terms of loving God and being loved by him. Nonetheless, such a relationality with God can only be incidental to his being because the monadic ontology of Islam's deity precludes it from being essential to his being. Rarely do even Sufis speak of being loved *by* God. Even though some Sufis speak of their love *for* God, they recognize almost universally that God's transcendence means he would not have "feelings akin to their own." Margaret Smith, *Rabi'a the Mystic and her fellow saints in Islam* (Cambridge: Cambridge University Press, 2010), 92.

forever; in Islam it is to know God's power and be his vice-regent on earth (against the advice of the angels, remember).

There is a tradition among some Muslims that on the day of judgment Muhammad will intercede for other Muslims, and they will receive the mercy of God. This tradition, though, is foreign to the Qur'an wherein it is clearly stated that "All intercession belongs to God" (39:44). Indeed, in the Qur'an Allah himself ridicules those who suppose that intercession will prevail for them on that day, and will say to them: "You have come to Us each on his own, just as We created you the first time, and you have left behind what We had provided for you. We do not see with you your intercessors whom you claimed were partners among you. All your means have been cut off and that which you have claimed has deserted you" (6:94). This itself is a reiteration of an equally clear injunction to Muhammad earlier in the same surah: "And warn by the Qur'an those who fear that they will be gathered before their Lord—for them besides Him will be no protector and no intercessor—that they might become righteous" (6:51).

In yet another section we find Allah explicitly telling Muhammad that his intercession for a group of evil-doers is useless, "You have no concern in the affair whether He turns to them (mercifully) or chastises them, for surely they are unjust," and the following verse clarifies that this is a universal principle related not just to that particular community but to all the cosmos: "And whatever is in the heavens and whatever is in the earth is Allah's; He forgives whom He pleases and chastises whom He pleases; and Allah is Forgiving, Merciful" (3:128, 129). Whatever other traditions may exist, the Qur'an is overwhelmingly clear on this matter, "On that day, intercession will not benefit anyone other than the one whom the Almighty has granted permission and accepts what he has to say" (20:109).

Perhaps this monadic nature of God in Islam is also a clue as to why, in orthodox Islam, each person must stand, alone and naked, before Allah—because God is a monad each human, too, is accounted as a monad.

Christianity suggests something different: because God is trinity, all humanity is a family having some degree of collective responsibility. As Paul put it: "For as in Adam all die, so also in Christ shall all be made alive" (1 Corinthians 15:22). Because the One God is a community of persons, and we are made in his image and likeness, we all can be harmed by each other and also blessed by each other. As the persons of the one God are, so is humanity, experiencing itself interdependently in a porosity and vulnerability making it possible that atonement be vicarious and not, as in Islam, merely private.[19]

Rituals

I suspect that we often see the heart of a religion much more in its rituals and lived practices than its official doctrines. I remember hearing at university that the words *ritual, rite, truce* and *truth* are all from the same ancient Indo-European root. My dictionary's etymology doesn't go back any further than Old English and German, but I find the idea compelling because a rite is a revelation of truth, an enactment of truth. People with little cognitive understanding of the doctrines may vigorously participate in the rituals of the two communities. Where they are limited because of class, education, sex, or what have you, there is usually room for a personal ritual. I think here of women in Egypt sitting around and reciting the entire Qur'an over bottles of water to bless it. They might be able to attend the local mosque *if it has a room for women*, but some don't, so here is a ritual they have devised on their own.

We will now briefly visit the central rituals that materially express truth in these two metanarratives. Indeed, a ritual is in some way a retelling or reenactment of some part of the metanarrative, and thus becomes a participation in it.

In Christianity we have two primary sacraments, sometimes also called mysteries or ordinances. These were explicitly commanded by Jesus and so are called "dominical," from the Latin word for "Lord." First is Baptism. In giving his Church its mission to go to the ends of the world and make disciples, he also taught them how to incorporate new converts or believers into that Church: Baptism in the name of the Father, Son, and the Holy Spirit (Matthew 28:19). Baptism is a reenactment of the deliverance

---

19   Islam certainly has a doctrine of atonement, but one can only atone for one's owns sins, as is the case in the one who dies waging jihad. But Shi'ites have a doctrine of redemptive suffering in Husayn, who is believed to have been a "ransom for his people, for Mankind." John L. Esposito, *Islam: the Straight Path* (3d ed.;Oxford: Oxford University Press,1988), 260-63.

of the Hebrews through the Red Sea, which itself was pointing to Jesus' death and resurrection. Baptism is a passing from the kingdom of this world to the Kingdom of God, from death to life, from worship of false idols (including one's self) to the worship of God, and from sin to righteousness. It is the outward sign of repentance, which is both how one enters the Kingdom of God and prepares for its coming.

Communion, also called the Lord's Supper or Eucharist (Greek for *thanksgiving*), is a ritual that has three tenses. It is a memorial of the past in that we remember Jesus' death. It is the reception of "true food" and "true drink" (John 6:55) that strengthens us now to carry out the mission he has given us. And it is focused on the future in that it announces that Christ will someday return to judge the living and dead, and his Kingdom will have no end.

In Islam we have the five pillars. I will be very brief with these because usually, if people know anything about Islam from school or college, this is familiar territory.

The first one is reciting the *shahada*—"there is no deity but Allah and Muhammad is his apostle or messenger." This affirms two of the doctrines I just discussed above: God as monadic unity and Muhammad as Seal of the Prophets. This very brief confession is roughly analogous to the Apostles' Creed in Christianity, for in each community these respective professions contain the basic truths one must confess in order to become a member.[20]

The second pillar is *zakat*, or alms. This is a percentage of one's worth (not income) given once a year (usually); traditionally it must be used to help Muslims but not non-Muslims. This reinforces the sense of brotherhood among Muslims throughout the world.

Third, we have *hajj*, or pilgrimage. This is the pilgrimage to Mecca to circumambulate the Ka'ba and engage in some other rituals there. All Muslims are supposed to take part in this at least once during their lifetime. If you are too sick or old to do this, you can hire someone to do it for you. Many people who go on hajj experience a sense of grandeur at how varied the Muslim *umma* is, with rich and poor coming from China, Argentina, Canada, India, Kenya, and nearly every country in the world.

---

20   Though in Islam, a male must be circumcised if he is not already.

There is a general understanding that upon the completion of the hajj one's past sins are completely forgiven.

Fourth is *salat*, or prayers. These are to be said five times a day. There is greater merit if you say these prayers in a mosque, though they can be said at home or in a business place. Prayers were originally performed facing Jerusalem, but after Muhammad had his falling out with the Jews of Yathrib it was changed to Mecca. Before doing the prayers people generally engage in a ritual cleansing. *Salat* normally consists of formal prayers and recitations from parts of the Qur'an. It must always be done in Arabic, though the Friday sermon (*xutba*) may be done in the local language.[21] After the *salat* if a person has individual things to ask from God (wisdom, a wife, a job, rain) there are some brief formalized petitions he can recite.[22] One thing about *salat* in the mosque that is worth mentioning is that you don't choose where you sit. No matter who you are, you take the next place in line and this could (theoretically) mean a beggar praying next to a king or president. I find this aspect of *salat* rather beautiful.

Finally, there is fasting or *sawm*. This is to be done during the lunar month of Ramadan, though most Muslims don't know why this is the case. The Islamic calendar is lunar, but unlike the Hebrew calendar it doesn't get an extra month every couple of years, so Ramadan shifts slowly through the seasons. The fast, which lasts from sunup to sundown, requires that you not swallow anything at all, even saliva. When the days are long and the weather is hot this can be extremely taxing. At the end of Ramadan, families may buy clothes or toys for the kids, and every day during Ramadan large feasts at sun down are common. It is usually a happy time for Muslims in spite of the fasting.

Concluding remarks

Are there parallels between Christianity and Islam in these issues? Muslims fast during Ramadan and Christians fast during Lent. The nature of the fast is different and in Christianity varies greatly from place to place.

---

21   While a sermon may accompany the prayers, the sermon itself is not a pillar of Islam.
22   Somewhat like the collects in the *Book of Common Prayer*, but sometimes even briefer.

But keeping some sort of fast is valuable, edifying, and biblical. Christians have the tradition of tithing, or giving ten percent of their income to charity or the Church, though there is no teaching that this money must go only or primarily to Christians. And Christians do go on pilgrimage, though it is not mandatory. I lived for years in Nazareth, and every day you'd see Christians from Africa, India, Europe, Latin America and everywhere in between walking down Pope Paul VI Street to visit the spring where Mary got water (and that must have been the real place, because you can't really move a spring or forget where it is), and then to the house of Mary (maybe the real place, and if not, very close to the real place), and then up to Mount Precipice off of which they were going to throw Jesus (Luke 4:29). Once I was heading to Jerusalem from Amman and I told my young taxi driver that I was going to visit our holiest place at the Church of the Resurrection (or the Church of the Holy Sepulcher, as the Western Christians call it) and I would like to know how I could intercede for him there. He almost started to cry because he was so moved by this. He told me he would like to get married and when I was there I interceded for him.

After living in the Middle East for most of a decade, I must say that I find the public religion of Muslims (and Eastern Orthodox Christians) compelling and refreshing. Yes, sometimes it can be confrontational, but the introspective Christianity of the West with its quietism and compartmentalization strikes me as defeatist, bland, and feeble-hearted. I am not saying that Christians should engage in public acts of religion for the sake of gaining the praise of people (Jesus clearly disliked this), but why not tell people "merry Christmas" instead of "Happy holidays"? Why not go caroling in your neighborhood and sing songs about baby Jesus? Why not process publicly, with cross and vestments and all, while singing hymns, to a nearby church or around your neighborhood? Why shouldn't pastors and priests wear clerical clothing in public? And why shouldn't nuns and monks show their unique, powerful vocations by dressing differently? Keeping religion out of the public square and government is deeply unbiblical and harmful to our societies, and if it takes Muslims to remind us of that, so be it.[23]

---

23 One reader responded that the separation of religion and politics is in the constitution. Not true. The constitution says that there shall be no established state church—very different.

Let's summarize what has been presented to this point: Christianity begins with a God who creates humans who misuse their free will (sin), and death then infects the entire universe. Humans are not able to repair the universe, or even their own relationships, but God endeavors to do just this. He elects the man Abraham and promises that he will be the conduit of God's blessing to the nations of the world. The blessing of God reaches its culmination in the person of Jesus Christ who in his own body and person has brought the reign of God into this broken world, and he announces that people everywhere should prepare for the unveiling of this hidden Kingdom by repenting. The promise to Abraham that God's blessing would extend to all the nations of earth requires that this message be global in its scope, and so the Church is founded—the logic of the Covenant with Abraham and Jesus' summons to repentance give birth to this community.

In Islam, the fundamental problem is not death, but ignorance to the context of this eternal contest between the Devil and God. People are basically good, born into submission (*Islam*) to their Creator. Prior revelations of God's instructions for life and society have been distorted, or lost, or abrogated. Therefore, the final revelation from the seal of the prophets is needed. This is Muhammad, who in his Qur'an and his every deed and word shows forth the eternal will of God for all human society and conduct. The eternal wisdom and will of God has now been decisively revealed, and his community, the Umma, is given the divine mandate to spread this message to the ends of the earth, enjoining the good, and forbidding the wrong.

This all leads us to the next question: how well are these two communities doing as they attempt to carry out their respective missions? To this question we now turn.

Discussion Questions

....

The author argues that Islam and Christianity are the greatest forces in influencing humanity over the last millennium, and will continue to be. Do you agree or disagree? What are some other contenders for this role?

Seven

THE STATE OF THE MISSION

In this book, we have examined the metanarratives of Islam and Christianity. This is not the same thing, precisely, as giving the histories of Islam and Christianity, as I have tried to clarify. And now we can focus on asking the question: how are these two communities doing at fulfilling their missions today? At the same time, we will ask: how are these two communities fulfilling their missions? As with most other topics this cannot claim to be comprehensive.

The Church: Making disciples of all nations

The mission of the Church is stipulated very clearly (and famously) in Matthew 28:18-20:

> And Jesus came and said to them, "All authority in heaven and on earth has been given to me.
> **Go** therefore
> and **make disciples** of all nations,
> **baptizing them** in the name of the Father and of the Son and of the Holy Spirit,
> **teaching them** to observe all that I have commanded you.
> And behold, I am with you always, to the end of the age."

Jesus starts by stating that, like the Son of Man figure from Daniel, he has now received all authority in heaven and on earth (Daniel 7:13 and following). This is the basis for Jesus giving them this mission. In the resurrection God has publicly demonstrated that Jesus has been given all authority in heaven and on earth. It is on the basis of this power that he is sending out these disciples of his. The command is to go, and it is only one command. Now, *as they are going* they are to do three things: make disciples, Baptize new converts, and teach them the fullness of Jesus' message. These three activities are to characterize the way in which they go into all the world.

Making disciples presumably starts before conversion. Otherwise the order of the three elements loses its coherence. They make disciples, and then if a disciple wishes to pledge his life and eternity to Jesus and this Kingdom, he is baptized into the name of the Trinity. And then, after this initiation of Baptism, they are to be taught the entirety of the content of Jesus' message—ethical, ritual, theological, social, political, and familial. This going into to *all nations* is central because as soon as the Church stops going and starts simply staying put, its contribution to the fulfillment of God's covenant with Abraham to bless *all the nations* of the world ends.

Jesus' promise to be with his Church is completely connected to its obedience to this command. It is not surprising then to see that the churches that are least involved in evangelism and foreign missions to the unreached are those that are dying, including all the mainline Churches in the USA—the Presbyterian Church of the USA, the Evangelical Lutheran Church of America, my own Episcopal Church of the USA, the United Methodist Church, and so on.

So far we have seen what Jesus had in mind when he founded a community and a movement, the one we today call the Church. But now we reach the part in the Christian metanarrative in which *we* are living. It is true that we are skipping 1900+ years of Church history. We could explore to what extent the church in different places and at different times remained faithful to its *raison d'être*. But this historical exploration is beyond the scope of this work. Rather, let us ask how the Church is doing 2000 years on—*today*?

As a professor I would give the Church a "C." Passing, certainly, but not with much distinction. The first thing the modern reader needs to understand is that "nations" in the Great Commission does not mean "nation states." That is, the purpose of the Church is not merely to make sure that each nation state has a local church. Nation states are an invention of modernity, and this way of ordering the population and territory of the earth is not working well in many places such as Afghanistan, Iraq, Somalia, Libya, and Yemen among others.

If "nations" doesn't mean "nation states," then what does it mean? Roughly, it means all the peoples, or ethnic groups, or social groupings of the world. It does not focus on individuals, but recognizes the reality that the proclamation of the Kingdom of God must take root in each ethnic-cultural grouping throughout the world. Furthermore, this is related to the impending eschaton[1] and is the appropriate and necessary condition for the entering of the Kingdom into human history in its fullness: "And this gospel of the kingdom will be proclaimed throughout the whole world as a testimony to all *nations,* and then the end will come." (Matthew 24:14). Here the reality of the authority of the Son of Man and the global reach of the Kingdom are united in the preaching of the community of the New Covenant—the Church.

In sum, regarding the terms *peoples* and *nations,* we are talking about groupings of people who share a similar culture, language, and identity. It doesn't mean they are all the same, but the point is that the Gospel message can flow freely within a people group. And it is Jesus' vision that his Kingdom and message extend to each and every people group. There is no indication that it has to become predominant, or victorious, or powerful in each group, but rather that he should have at least a handful of disciples from "every nation and tribe and language and people" (Revelation 14:6).

His vision for how this will happen is discipleship, as explained above. Discipleship, in this progression, often begins *before* conversion. This was Jesus' own practice, as the New Testament is pretty clear that the disciples didn't fully grasp the Gospel until after the resurrection and, indeed, after Pentecost. There is nothing wrong with having a coordinated discipleship program at a given church, but discipleship at its most basic level is really about learning the Christian faith and life by spending time with a more mature Christian, and learning by observation. I was not raised in a Christian household, and it was not until I was about 11 or 12 that I started

---

1   See the glossary for more on this word.

to go to church. This was in Puebla, México, and our small Bible church had a Mexican pastor, but our youth pastor was an American missionary from San Antonio (I would later marry a young lady from the church in San Antonio that had sent the youth pastor out as a missionary). He was enthusiastic about discipleship and we would meet once a week to study the Scriptures, but I would also run errands with him, and have meals with him and his family. This was my first exposure to a Christian family. I don't really remember much from our Bible studies (though I'm thankful that we had these), but being an only child from a divorced home that was, in retrospect, pretty dysfunctional, this was amazing to me.

He and his wife respected each other, and he had children who respected him. He did not assume that they should do so because "he was the man," but because he worked hard to provide for them and to be an example for them. This was all very radical and countercultural for a young American who had always learned what all contemporary American boys learn: that men are inferior to women and that husbands and fathers are easily dispensable. This was the fruit of discipleship, and it is offered here as an example of what making disciples looked like at one point in my own life.

Later on, when I was studying philosophy at the University of Texas at San Antonio, I was asked to be the student president of the local chapter of InterVarsity Christian Fellowship. We were a medium-sized group with maybe sixty or so people who were regularly involved. We had a prayer group, some small groups that met in students' homes, and a large group celebration each week. I accepted the invitation to take up this position from our staff worker, and I thought, now what am I going to do? One thing I decided to do was focus on discipleship, and I invited three young men to meet with me on a regular basis, to talk, pray, study, and even just run errands together. I don't know how much of an impression that semester left on them, but the point is that I was emulating what my first teacher had done. This is the principle we see here in the Great Commission.[2]

There is a real problem, though. If disciples are going to be made among all the peoples of the world, then someone needs to actively get up and go to those people groups that have no disciples—we call these

---

2   A similar instruction is found in 2 Tim 2:2.

unreached people groups. There are some such unreached people groups in the USA, but most of them are in the majority-Muslim, Hindu, and Buddhist regions. In some of these unreached regions the local churches are reaching out, like in China and India. But there are other parts of the world where the Church is declining; here I think of the Middle East, where ancient and large churches in Turkey, Lebanon, Syria, Iraq, Persia, Egypt, Israel-Palestine, Jordan, Arabia, and the Maghreb have either been exterminated totally, or are in a state of steady or rapid decline. Christians tend to make much of the very real fact that Muslims there are converting to Christianity. This is true, but for every convert to Christianity from Islam who stays in the Middle East, there are more indigenous Christians who flee to the West out of security concerns.

Also, the American Church spends almost no money fulfilling Jesus' great commission to his disciples. The tens of thousands of unreached people groups just mentioned are just not on the radar of most American churches. Americans certainly spend a lot on "missions," but this almost always means sending money and/or people *to fellow Christians* who are poor. As laudable as this may be, it does not advance the Great Commission at all.

Another error is to suppose that because there are Christians in, say, India, that the Great Commission has been fulfilled there: India is a nation and it has been reached, but this is wrong. The modern concept of the nation state with its defined borders and passports is utterly foreign to the world of the Bible.[3] In the Bible the nations are the Amorites, Egyptians, Persians, Arabs, Greeks, and, unnamed though they may be, the Aztecs, Hausa, Cheyenne, and Sioux. This is the Biblical template for the Church's mission: making sure that each of these tribes has disciples who are making disciples. If a local church becomes aware of a tribe or people group, whether near or far, that has no disciples, it takes upon itself the cross-cultural mission of making disciples.

All of this reveals that there is a real problem with how many Christians in the West think about missions—indeed I would go so far as to say that the predominant missiology of most American churches is completely

---

3   And with modernity, I expect that the 'nation state' will continue to decline in power and cohesion and importance in favor of trans-national networks and local, tribal groups. This theory regarding the future of global politics is called neo-medievalism.

foreign to anything found in Scripture. Just ask your own church: do we support financially any missionaries working with the 1/3 of the world population that is unreached? The answer will almost certainly be *no*.

Consider these sobering figures, based on the research of Gordon-Conwell Theological Seminary's respected Center for the Study of Global Christianity:

Basically, the world can be divided into three parts based on how people respond to two questions:

1. Do you have access to a Christian witness?
2. Are you a Christian?

People that respond "yes" to both questions are considered "World C". These people are spread out in countries like the United States, Spain, England, Poland, Kenya, Romania, and all throughout Latin America. They have had significant access to the gospel and many people living in these areas would at least claim to be "Christian" even though they may be very nominal or cultural followers of Christ. About 10% of the world's population is estimated to be true believers while another 23% are at least considered adherents to the Christian faith.

People that respond "yes" to the first question and "no" to the second question are considered "World B". These people are spread throughout countries like India, Thailand, Japan, China, Nigeria, and Vietnam. These are people that for the most part have had access to the gospel but have not chosen to embrace it for any number of reasons. They are what we would call exposed unbelievers because they have had a chance to respond to the message.

People that responded "no" to both questions are considered "World A". These people live in countries like Iran, Bhutan, Somalia, Turkey, Afghanistan, and Algeria. Many of these people have no access to a Christian, a missionary, a church, or a Bible. These individuals are virtually unreached and would need an outside witness to come and share Christ with them. We refer to them as unexposed unbelievers because they have not had any real chance of hearing about Jesus.

As of 2011, the world's population can be divided into these three categories:

- World A – 1.6 billion people 29.6% of the world's population
- World B – 2.4 billion people 40.1% of the world's population
- World C – 2.0 billion people 33.0% of the world's population

So, where are the missionaries going?

This is the breakdown of the worldwide foreign missionary force and where they are currently deployed:

- World A – 10,200 (2.4%)
- World B – 103,000 (24.5%)
- World C – 306,000 (73.1%)

So, basically, we only have 2.4% or 1 out of every 40 of our foreign missionaries serving among "World A" where the majority of the unreached people groups in the world live.[4]

The findings above are not very positive. The churches in America are very busy, but obviously they are not busy fulfilling the great commission. Perhaps they do not understand that it is the very reason they exist.

In any case, such findings lead me to doubt that the Churches of the West (excepting some Pentecostal ones) will recover a Biblical vision of mission and discipleship. They are branches that will be cut off from the vine and they will die. They are doing good things, like serving at soup kitchens and helping the homeless—these are important facets of the Church's *domestic* work.[5] But they are not fulfilling their final cause or *telos*, which is the Great Commission. They have this mind frame that says, "There is so much work to be done *here*, why do we need to go overseas?" This is a profoundly anti-Jesus and anti-Scripture sort of thing to say. I always ask people who talk like this, "What about your pagan ancestors? You would still be pagan had it not been for these people who had the courage to 'Go' like Jesus said—Paul, Patrick, Augustine, Frumentius, David of Wales, Ninian, Boniface, Francis Xavier, Andrew. Did they not 'have a lot to do here?'"

But it is not all bad news. Some great things have happened in the last

---

4   From globalfrontiermissions.org/state-of-the-world-the-task-remaining/, accessed
    6 January 2015. Reprinted with permission.
5   The word *domestic* is derived from the Greek word for *home*: it is the work you do in
    your own house or home. By extension, American churches do a lot of work in their
    home and never go outside.

century or so. China is a bright spot—with surprising growth. Africa was about 10% Christian in 1900 and by 2000 it was 40% Christian. Pentecostalism, despite its propensity to cults of personality and certain excesses, has been a great gift to the Church's *missio ad gentes*.[6] I have devoted much of my study[7] to understanding Christian conversion from Islam, and it is true that there has been a large upswing in the number of such converts since roughly the 1960s. I also have to say, though, that despite the hype surrounding this reality, I don't think it's going to make a huge difference on a global scale. Even if the number of converts doubled next year, it would still be a small drop in the bucket of the 22% of the world population that is the Islamic *umma*.

Europe is a hard nut to crack. I was very much a fan of Pope Benedict XVI's vision for the re-evangelization of Europe. Indeed, I suspect this is why he took the name of Benedict, St Benedict of Nursia being the patron saint of Europe. But the state churches there are largely useless and we should not be surprised if they continue to shrivel up and die. So many of those established churches are indistinguishable in their rhetoric and activity from the voices of the secular left. Very few of these churches actively proclaim the hard realities which neither Jesus nor the Apostles avoided: the reality and gravity of sin, the depth of the human's alienation from God and his neighbor, and the utter inability of humans to create their own paradise here on earth. In the words of Francis Schaeffer, "Tell me what the world is saying today, and I'll tell you what the Church will be saying in seven years."[8]

If Europe has any hope, it is in two areas: Pentecostalism and traditionalist Catholicism. Europe has received large numbers of Pentecostal immigrants from Africa, Latin America, and the Caribbean. Some of the largest congregations in Europe are of the Pentecostal variety, and these churches, unlike the failed experiments of magisterial Protestantism, are thriving. There is something about Pentecostal Christianity which allows the Christian to be at home in modernity while not imbibing to the dregs

---

6   Latin for 'mission to the peoples [of the world]'. I wonder if God made the Azusa Street Revival happen in 1906 precisely because the mainline churches were just not doing their part in fulfilling the *missio ad gentes*.

7   See my doctoral dissertation on this: Duane Alexander Miller, *Living among the Breakage: Contextual Theology-making and ex-Muslim Christians*, Pickwick, 2016.

8   Schaeffer is alleged to have said shortly before his death in 1984, and it has been widely cited in quality publications, but as far as I can tell it was not a written text.

the spirit of the age (as have done the state churches). There is no doubt that Pentecostals sometimes struggle with things like the pastor's cult of personality and a flawed theology of wealth, but the fundamental meta-narrative of the faith is taught and proclaimed by their churches.

Traditionalist Catholics also are an occasion for hope. The parts of the Catholic Church that have become enamored of the god of this age will continue to diminish according to the inscrutable and benevolent providence of God. Traditionalist Catholics who are unapologetic about their unicity and peculiarity in reference to not only the world, but also to other Christian communities, and who have appropriated the rich heritage of their Church's spirituality, discipline, theology, and ethics—these are men and women who will "be fruitful and multiply" while also being equipped to undermine and demolish the metaphysically jejune and axiologically arbitrary structures of the secular age. In sum, I see a future for Pentecostals and traditionalist Catholics in Europe, while the magisterial Protestant churches will continue their inexorable and irreversible decline. This analogy should not be missed: a Europe with no hope fails to produce enough children to avoid self-genocide; the European churches with no gospel must follow the same path.

The good news is that while many of the Churches in the USA and Europe will slowly die out, the individual Christian can do a great deal. Find a missionary to support—someone reaching out to *unreached people groups*. Pick up a copy of *Operation World* and pray for the Church's mission in all the various parts of the world, that book will give you details on the needs and status of the Church's *missio ad gentes* there. Or, get involved in your own congregations' missions/outreach committee, and be a voice for fulfilling the Great Commission. My experience tells me that people will dislike you when you do this because it runs contrary to their own inclinations, which usually revolve around having "missions" as an activity offered to people in the congregation, or as one priest called it, a vacation with a halo. These short-term missions (STM) alone will *never* result in a people group going from unreached to reached.[9] This is not the biblical understanding of the mission of the Church at all. So, for the

---

9   Reached meaning that the people group has an indigenous church, with indigenous leadership, and is operating sacramentally. In other words, they are now able to make disciples of their own people.

reader who will actually take up this challenge, be prepared for opposition. You are going to a committee of well-intentioned Christians who are sure that they are doing the work of God, have been told by their pastor they are doing a great job, and you are bearing the bad news that their understanding of the Church's mission is much too small. As T. S. Eliot wrote, "Humankind cannot bear very much reality."[10]

At the end of the day, truth is important to the Church, and the truth is that "missions" is not just one of many activities a local parish may or may not offer. If what I'm saying is true, a church that does not fulfill its role in the Great Commission will die. Jesus is Lord of the Church, and we find the vision in Revelation chapters 1–2 of Jesus informing various city-churches that their place in his lamp stand is in danger. They are told what they need to fix in order to secure their place. Churches of the West: you have been warned.

Above I pointed to Pentecostals and traditionalist Catholics as communities that retain a liveliness and vivacity that will help them to avoid the extinction which the state churches have chosen. There are some other causes for optimism which we can point to in reference to Western Christianity—ones that indicate a resistance to the shallow understanding of "missions as church activities." Here are, in brief, some examples of communities or movements that retain the biblical vision of mission as *telos* of the Church:

- The Lausanne Movement: Based on the Lausanne Covenant of 1974, an evangelical movement that is committed to a church for every people group in the world, this movement has managed to blend action and the production of a wealth of articles and conferences on the Church's global mission.
- Eight editions of *Operation World*: a book that lists, in alphabetical order, all the countries of the world. Each country listing has some basic information on population and religion, and then the reader is given some prayer points. This sort of tool can transform a little prayer meeting into a force for world mission as they pray with knowledge for the Church's mission in Azerbaijan, Mongolia, and Yemen.

---

10   From *Burnt Norton* (1935) in his *Four Quartets*.

- A new generation of missionary societies: As the urgency of the Church's mission to the unreached became more apparent, a new generation of missionary societies devoted to that ministry were born. In many cases the established missionary societies had become ossified and unwilling to engage in the creative and daring task of evangelism among Buddhists, Hindus, and Muslims. *Frontiers, New Tribes Mission* and *Anglican Frontier Missions* are three examples of such new mission societies.
- The 10/40 window: a phrase that was coined by evangelist Luis Bush in 1990, and refers to the regions of the world located between 10° and 40° north of the equator, encompassing North Africa, the Middle East, and much of South and South East Asia. This region was identified as being in particular need of evangelism and mission because so many of the people groups there are unevangelized. The 10/40 window helped mission agencies and churches to prioritize mission to the unreached.

These are a few examples that indicate a liveliness among some of the Christians of the West in relation to the correct and biblical understanding of mission, over and against the misunderstanding of "mission as a church activity."

In conclusion, after 2,000 years, thousands of people groups around the world do not have disciples, and the churches in the West seem to show little to no interest in actually doing what Jesus said. There is, though, enough obedience to Jesus on the fringes of American Christianity and in the two-thirds world to keep this mission from failing outright. So, like I said, I give the contemporary Church a grade of C in her fulfillment of the great commission.

The Umma: Living the shari'a

The Qur'an says of the *umma*:

Ye are the **best of peoples**, evolved for mankind, enjoining what is right, forbidding what is wrong, and believing in Allah. If only the People of the Book had faith, it were best for them: among them are

some who have faith, but most of them are perverted transgressors.
(3:110, Yusuf Ali)

The *umma* has its mission of spreading the truth around the world, there
are three primary ways it has of doing this, and we see them directly in
the Qur'an: jihad (holy war), migration, and da'wa (inviting a person to receive Islam). The purpose of the *umma* is to continue its work until there is
no one who does not confess the truth that there is no deity but Allah and
that Muhammad is his apostle. Not all Muslims in a community will be
directly devoted in the accumulation of political power in order to assist
the *umma* in its divine mission of enjoining the right and forbidding the
wrong, but some will. Indeed, the Islamic metanarrative requires it once
the *umma*'s presence makes this possible.

From a Muslim point of view this is a beautiful vision, and non-Muslims need to grasp this. Islam is the natural religion, restoring lost knowledge to men about the ideal, pure, and good way of living. A Muslim might
say, "Imagine how peaceful and good the world will be when there is one
successor (caliph) to Muhammad ruling over the entire world, according
to the benevolent and objective eternal shari'a of God. It may be true that
jihad is sometimes necessary to secure that beautiful future of truth, prosperity, and peace, but that is the nature of life. And besides, Muslims who
die in jihad do not need to worry about whether or not they will enter
paradise, for they have a firm guarantee from God that they will."[11]

Jihad

Regarding jihad, it is true that there is also a sort of spiritual jihad, but
no one in the West is bothered by that. On the other hand, we have the
authoritative, *abrogating* surahs of the Qur'an that speak very highly of
what is plainly a coercive and military jihad. So the question is then, when
is jihad permitted and/or mandatory? This is where one will have many
different ideas from different scholars. Most Muslims will agree that jihad
is permitted (if not mandatory) in the West Bank, which they see as a
Muslim society that is being occupied by the Israeli military. I don't think

---

11   4:74

that is particularly negative regarding Islam, because almost anyone, anywhere in the world, would fight to control what they believe to be their own homeland.

We have already seen how Bin Laden argued that 9/11 was a legitimate act of self-defense, an effort to harm the financial and political engines of the persecutors of the *umma*. While many Muslims do not accept this argument, it is compelling to many others, and for them there is nothing unreasonable about it at all. They might point out, for instance, that in WW2 the Allies destroyed many targets that were not immediately related to the Axis militaries. Furthermore, Bin Laden did not accept the modernist imposition of artificial "nation states" upon the world map. For him, an attack against Muslims anywhere is, *ipso facto*, an attack against the *umma*, nation state boundaries are arbitrary.

To build a Christian analogy from history: the basis for the medieval order was Christendom, which was clearly not one nation state, so when the Arabs took Jerusalem from the Byzantine Empire (a member of Christendom), all of Christendom was offended. This is why it was a cause of just war for Christendom to go (rather belatedly) and take Jerusalem back from the Arab Saracens, who had taken it away from them in a wanton war of aggression.

All of this to say, if we favor the negative view, held by some Muslims, of Christians and Jews as unbelievers, then it is at least comprehensible to look at the world through the traditional Islamic vision of the Abode of Islam *(dar al islam)*, the House of War *(dar al harb)*, and then the areas that are not yet ruled by Islam but have a temporary peace pact with it *(dar al hudna)*. There is no way to figure out precisely how the world's Muslim population understands the difference between terrorism and a legitimate jihad.

Because this is distasteful and politically incorrect in Western societies, Muslim public figures in the West talk about Islam as a religion of peace. For instance, I have seen imams on the television quoting peaceful verses from the Qur'an, assuring the host of the news program of the compatibility of Islam with secular modernity. But I think both the imam and I know that verse is abrogated! That is, the tolerant-sounding verse has been cancelled or modified by a later revelation that is more antagonistic or violent. But everyone in the television audience feels better and happy.

The imam may indeed hope for the eventual triumph of Islam over the decadent culture of the West (I certainly would expect him to), and he might teach this in private. But he is not likely to say this publicly when his community stands nothing to gain from such an admission.

Yes, Islam is a religion of peace inasmuch as it envisions a final state of peace when the whole world is under the leadership of Muhammad's successor and the entire world is living according to God's benevolent shari'a. Until then jihad may be permitted or even commanded. It is the mission and purpose of the *umma* to enforce the good of the shari'a and prohibit that which is bad according to it.

All of this to say, there is no clear way to gauge how Muslims interpret jihad. Also, it is irrational and unreasonable to look at acts of what people call "terrorism" and say, without really understanding the thinking of the alleged terrorist, "That is not Islam." It certainly has a therapeutic value in that it might make people feel better, but it's not responsible and is in fact disrespectful to people who make great sacrifices (even their own lives) in order to carry out what they sincerely believe to be their creator's will.

There is no precise parallel in Christianity, but by way of comparison, consider the successful Christian professional who leaves his job to be a missionary in a dangerous part of the world and ends up being killed. Other Christians might regard his zeal as unreasonable or reckless, but no one should say that Christianity was not in fact what motivated and inspired him.

The use of terms like fundamentalism, radicalism, extremism, and terrorism is an inauthentic act that we use in order to not face the hard question: what if that is authentic Islam? In my experience almost every time a person uses a word like that it is in order to differentiate between the good guys and the bad guys, but when the person using the word is challenged to provide a careful definition of the word, they are not able to do so. These words, then, are more a gauge of the subjectivity of the one using them than adjectives describing objective reality.[12]

---

12   This is not to say that no academic attempts have been made to carefully define terrorism. See, for instance, William J Abraham, *Shaking Hands with the Devil: The Intersection of Theology and Terrorism.* My point is that people use this word all the time without having really thought about it.

Da'wa

On to da'wa, which is an Arabic word meaning *calling*, as in "calling people to Islam." This is more or less like evangelism for Christians and is considered a highly regarded Muslim deed. Muslim communities throughout the West are often quite active in portraying a very positive vision of Islam and inviting people explicitly to embrace it. This is one way that Islam in the West is clearly superior to Christianity in the West. So many Churches will feed Muslims, teach them the local language, educate their children, clothe them, and meet their needs, but never invite them to embrace Christianity. I'm not saying that help from Christians should be contingent on conversion (though in Islamic da'wa that is indeed permitted), but our ministries exist to show people, in action, the Good News. And if we do not present the real, explicit offer to enter that Kingdom, then we are deciding to *not be* biblical and apostolic, for the New Testament is full of explicit and clear summons to make a decision about this Kingdom.

Is there evidence of permanent conversions to Islam on a large scale? Not really. But there certainly are converts: a woman who marries a Muslim man, a man who wants to marry a Muslim woman, college students, and prisoners. Many women are attracted to the vision of a traditional nuclear family with clear gender roles, and many churches today don't emphasize the beauty and sacredness of the nuclear family. Upon examining the rhetoric of some denominations in the West, there is such an emphasis on the heroic struggle of the single mother and all-consuming interest with same-sex marriage that one might easily come to the conclusion that the traditional nuclear family is in fact retrograde and unwelcome. Little wonder that young women who want a family look to the *umma* for validation of their desire for a traditional family. People are sometimes alarmed by the hijab, but when you compare it to how some young ladies dress, even in church on Sunday, we must admit that sometimes Muslims are more Biblical than we Christians! Our hypersexualization of young girls in the West is deeply destructive. We need to come to terms with that so we can have an honest conversation about women's rights and the role of girls and women in society. We also need to come to terms with the reality that the traditional Christian vision of womanhood is presently countercultural.

Another reason that some Christians (and secular Americans) are attracted to Islam is that it offers them a place in God's great plan for the world. That is, the metanarrative of Islam is quite masculine and virile. Christianity in America has become quite emasculated and can be summarized by, "Be nice to people, don't be judgmental, and don't talk about your religion." Much of the music sung in churches amounts to love songs for "Jesus, my boyfriend."[13] We should not be surprised that young men who want adventure and danger leave our churches. This problem is on the radar of some church leaders, and so we find books like *Why Men Hate Going to Church*[14] and *Men and the Church: is there a future?*[15] Islam: by men, for men. That is a great strength of Islam. Christianity had its bands of brothers (I think of the Society of Jesus, founded by a former soldier, which sent out young men to furthest reaches of the known world for the sake of the Church's *missio ad gentes*). Where are they now? Will the churches of the West be able to offer a positive and vital role for men in family, ministry, and government that values and fosters manliness?

When it comes to the nuclear family and men in the West, Muslims offer a coherent and traditional model. This model attracts men and women and may lead to conversion. I remember when my wife and I moved to Jordan with our young son. I was in my mid-20s and at first people assumed I was just a young American guy, traveling around, learning some Arabic, having a good time. But after people learned that not only was I married, but that I had a son, it was surprising how differently I was treated. Muslim men who were in their 40s or 50s treated me with respect, and a lot of that came from their culture wherein being a husband and father was respected. By way of contrast, in the USA some people seemed sad to hear that my wife had gotten pregnant so soon after getting married. The unstated sense was that we were really limiting ourselves by having a child so young—even though we had both completed university and were

---

13   I am indebted to a missionary friend of mine from the Reformed Church of America for
      this phrase. I wish I had thought of it. As his ministry is in a shari'a state his location
      cannot be disclosed.

14   David Murrow (Thomas Nelson, 2011)

15   Jay Crouse (Xulon, 2013)

employed. Muslims value fathers, husbands, and children; the West does not; therefore Islam has a future, and the West does not. But rather than rely on a few personal anecdotes let me unfold why the demographic dynamics at play in the West support this conclusion.

Fertility and Migration

The global percentage of Christians remained fairly stable between 1900 and 2014 moving slightly from 34.5% to 33%. The Muslim percentage, however, increased dramatically from about 12.34% to 23.04% during the same period.[16] Recent research from Pew predicts that Islam will become the largest religious block in the world, surpassing Christianity around 2070. This great increase does not come either from jihad or conversion. Rather, it comes from procreation. The future belongs to those who procreate. So here we need to start investigating a few realities related to migration and demographics. On the whole, my projection is that Europe will become increasingly Islamic, and by the end of the century many major cities will have Muslim pluralities (if not majorities). By plurality, I mean that Muslims form the largest segment of the population, not that Muslims are a majority of the population. So if you have a city that is 40% Muslim, 30% Christian, and 30% 'None', then you have a Muslim plurality. I also am limiting this projection to cities, which are the places that attract the majority of immigrants, as opposed to smaller towns and villages, which will, for the most part, be populated by the elderly European populations that are (nominally, at least) Christian. Furthermore, I want to limit these projections to Western Europe. The largest country in Europe is Russia, a country that is actively trying to counteract Islamization, unlike the countries of Western Europe.

Some time ago there was a rather ridiculous video posted on YouTube that talked about Muslims controlling all of Europe and the average Muslim woman having eight children. These figures are not substantiated and are clearly exaggerations. Once this was revealed by other researchers

---

16   Figures from here: www.gordonconwell.edu/resources/documents/
     StatusOfGlobalMission.pdf, accessed 3 January 2014.

there was a collective reaction of people thinking, "Phew! Thank goodness we don't have to worry about that!" The problem is that there was a seed of truth to that video, which was obviously exaggerated. What I want to do here is present some of the evidence that points to what I proposed above.

First, though, let me say that Christians should not really be sad about the decline of Western Civilization. It is true that Christianity helped to create the West, but the West under the influence of modernity has placed the individual human at the center of the universe (secular humanism), and not God or a vision for a Christian social-political order (Christendom). Therefore the West, for all of its positive and impressive achievements, has divorced itself from its origin, and so is leading an inauthentic and deracinated existence. Such a civilization cannot survive. Indeed, the West is actively and collectively deciding to discontinue its own existence by consistently, and on a dramatic scale, opting to not replace each generation with a subsequent generation of equal or greater size. Large families and the hedonism of secular humanism don't overlap. By hedonism I mean an ordering of life whereby pleasure (not truth, virtue, race, nation, or God) is considered to be the greatest good. Late modern humans tend to, without really thinking about it, default to some sort of hedonistic construction of values and meaning. The transcendental order of the cosmos of Christendom, for all its faults, rooted the West in something real; hedonistic humanism does not.

Islamic civilization (or civilizations) still place God at the center of the social and political order. The purpose of this book so far has been to contrast the Muslim vision for that social and political order from the Christian. But the Muslim vision for society is at least a positive[17] vision for the future, and marriage and children are certainly part of the Islamic vision of the good and fulfilling life, as they are for the lives of most Christians. As the West has become increasingly estranged from its Christian roots, though, it has lost the ability to objectively explain why marriage and children are good.

---

17 By saying it is positive here, I do need mean it is good. Rather, I mean it proposes an actual vision to work towards and build. Of course one can ask how attractive this future is for women and non-Muslims.

By way of contrast, an old Arabic proverb says, "Wealth and children are the adornment of the world" and in Genesis God blesses humans and says, "Be fruitful and multiply." Without God, why have children? Or specifically, why have more than two children—which would replace the man and the woman? Having *one* child is an interesting experience, and can fit into the hedonistic calculus of secular humanism. That is, there may be pleasure in the experience and novelty of having a child and engaging in the project of child-rearing. Having two children might give someone the experience of having one of each—a boy and a girl. But three children? There are no hedonistic reasons for this, especially when the pleasure of sex is, thanks to artificial birth control, completely divorced from the creation of new life.

This issue of motives for procreation ties into a culture's Total Fertility Rate (TFR). TFR refers to the average number of children born to a woman in her lifetime, assuming that woman lives to the end of her natural childbearing years (There are also other factors like net migration, child mortality, natural disasters, and wars which can have a dramatic effect on a country's population). A country needs a TFR of 2.1 to maintain a steady population (not taking into account migration). This means that the average woman will have two children and a few women will have three. This is necessary because some children die before reaching childbearing age. On the other hand, just because a population's TFR goes below 2.1 does not mean that it will *immediately* start shrinking. This is due to something called the tempo effect: "A tempo effect is defined as inflation or deflation of the period incidence of a demographic event (e.g., births, marriages, deaths) resulting from a rise or fall in the mean age at which the event occurs."[18] In other words, there is a period of lag between changes in fertility and a shrinking population.

Let's take a look at the TFR and populations of some key countries in the West, with the countries below replacement in italics:[19]

---

18   Elisabetta Barbi, "How long do we live? Demographic models and reflections on the tempo effects: An introduction", p 1.

19   The figures are from *index mundi* (indexmundi.com), accessed 23 December 2014.

COUNTRY	TFR	POPULATION
France	2.08	66 million
USA	2.06	314 million
UK	1.91	63 million
Netherlands	1.78	17 million
Australia	1.77	22 million
Denmark	1.74	5.5 million
Canada	1.59	34 million
Portugal	1.51	11 million
Spain	1.48	47 million
Austria	1.41	8.2 million
Germany	1.41	81 million
Italy	1.40	61 million

Only two of these countries are even *near* replacement level, the USA and France. Note, however, that TFR does not count children born to citizens, but children born to any woman, including immigrants, legal or otherwise, in that country. Without the fertility of immigrants in the West the TFR figures would be even lower.

Now let us take a look at the TFR figures for the fourteen most populous Muslim-majority countries in the world. (The TFR of small countries is important to the futures of those countries, but is not of special interest to us because a very high TFR for a country of, say, 100,000 people, is not likely to make a major impact on the world.)

COUNTRY	TFR	POPULATION	NET MIGRATION RATE PER 1000
Indonesia	2.23	249 million	-1.08
Pakistan	3.07	190 million	-2
Bangladesh	2.55	161 million	-1.04
Egypt	2.94	84 million	-0.2
Turkey	2.13	80 million	0.5
Iran	1.87	79 million	-0.11
Algeria	2.78	37 million	-0.27
Sudan	4.17	34 million	-4.52
Morocco	2.19	32 million	-3.67
Iraq	3.58	31 million	0
Afghanistan	5.64	30 million	-2.51
Uzbekistan	1.86	28 million	-2.65
Saudi Arabia	2.26	27 million	-0.64
Yemen	4.45	25 million	0

Only two of these countries are below TFR. Some are roughly at re-placement, but most of them are well above replacement levels.

If you look at the top ten countries in the world in terms of TFR, *all* of them are either Muslim-majority or in Sub-Saharan Africa.[20] Not until you get to the 52nd most fertile country in the world (Guatemala at 3.18) do you find a country in the Americas, and not until the 109th place do you find a country which is (often considered a) part of Europe: Turkey at 2.13.

So what happens with these growing populations? Historically, when populations grow beyond what the natural environment can provide, there are a couple of options. One is famine or starvation, whereby ex-cess humans die because they do not have enough food. This is largely countered today by international efforts at famine relief. Another option is war, whereby one community conquers the land and natural resources of another group, in the process exiling/killing/enslaving members of that other population. A third option is migration, sometimes peaceful, some-times not. Our present map is deeply influenced by these different shifts: the Saxons of Germany entering England, or the Turkic people of Central Asia conquering Asia Minor, or the Arabs from the Arabian Gulf who conquered the Nile Valley and once-fertile North Africa. For the most part, our international world order today means that refugees from local wars will not die, but be resettled, many of them in the West. Whether the war is civil or between two nation states, it matters not, for both types of wars cause displacement. Likewise, when there is a famine, instead of letting nature take its brutal and deadly course, we send famine relief. All of this leads to the inexorable reality that between the refugee resettle-ment system and the reality of migration (even if sometimes dangerous or illegal), some of the excess population from the fertile Muslim-majority countries will, sooner or later, end up in the West—in countries where the indigenous non-Muslim populations don't even *replace* their population

---

20   Many of the countries in Sub-Saharan Africa have large Christian majorities, and it is reasonable to expect world Christianity to look more and more African as the decades proceed. Already an African cardinal was considered to have a real chance at the pa-pacy; and the Archbishop of York, the second highest position in the Church of England after Canterbury, is African. African Anglicans have likewise launched missionary ventures in Europe and North America, and I know a number of local Christians whose bishop is African.

generation after generation. Witness the enormous numbers of Syrians migrating to Europe as a result of the civil war there.[21]

Now, let us take a look at migration patterns. Ideally, we would have data on what sort of migrants a country receives, what sort of migrants are leaving a country, and how many migrants are "just passing through." For instance, Turkey has many migrants who are on their way to Europe. Also, Iran has many *immigrants* from neighboring Afghanistan, resulting in a lower net figure. Egypt and the countries of North Africa, likewise, receive many people who are, or would like to be, *en route* to Europe, notably from chaotic and war torn places like Sudan and Somalia.

Now let us look at the net migration rates[22] for our Western countries:

COUNTRY	TFR	POPULATION	NET MIGRATION PER 1000
USA	2.06	314 million	3.62
Canada	1.59	34 million	5.65
UK	1.91	63 million	2.59
Italy	1.40	61 million	4.67
Austria	1.41	8.2 million	1.79
Germany	1.41	81 million	0.71
Denmark	1.74	5.5 million	2.36
Netherlands	1.78	17 million	2.02
France	2.08	66 million	1.1
Spain	1.48	47 million	5.02
Portugal	1.51	11 million	2.9
Australia	1.77	22 million	5.93

Obviously, not all of the immigrants to these countries are Muslims. On the other hand, there is no question that a substantial portion of them are. Consider these statistics from the Pew Forum:

---

21   I am aware of David Goldman's 2011 book *How Civilizations Die (and why Islam is Dying too)*, Washington, DC: Regnery. In this book he argues that while the West is dying, so is the Muslim world. He cites a number of countries in the Muslim world that have experienced steep reductions in fertility, like Iran and to a lesser extent Turkey. I enjoyed the book and the evaluations of Iran and Turkey were helpful. However, the author failed to deal with many of the countries in my list above. Furthermore, in many Muslim-majority countries fertility has indeed decreased, but it still remains well above replacement level. This means that they are not dying, just growing more slowly than in the past.

22   Note, however, that these migration rates were *before* the massive influx of migrants from Syria and other countries to Western Europe, and then especially Germany and Sweden, that started in 2015.

The number of Muslims in Europe has grown from 29.6 million in 1990 to 44.1 million in 2010. Europe's Muslim population is projected to exceed 58 million by 2030. Muslims today account for about 6% of Europe's total population, up from 4.1% in 1990. By 2030, Muslims are expected to make up 8% of Europe's population.[23]

This same study indicates that the Muslim population of Europe will continue to grow by over 1% a year through 2030, while the non-Muslim population, which is already in decline, as of 2020–2030 will continue to decline by .2% per year.

Let us now look at the projected percentage of Muslim population based on the Pew study and its projections:

COUNTRY	% MUSLIM IN 2010	% MUSLIM IN 2030
Austria	5.7%	9.3%
France	7.5%	10.3%
Germany	5.0%	7.1%
Italy	2.6%	5.4%
Spain	2.3%	3.7%
UK	4.6%	8.2%

What would these figures look like when extended out to 2100? It is difficult to find responsible projections for that figure, but a 2009 article from *The Telegraph* reports that about 20% of the EU population will be Muslim by 2050.[24] Muammar Gadhafi, one-time dictator of Libya, believed that Islam would become predominant in Europe within the century:

"We have 50 million Muslims in Europe," Gadhafi said. "There are signs that Allah will grant Islam victory in Europe – without swords, without guns, without conquests. The 50 million Muslims of Europe will turn it into a Muslim continent within a few decades."[25]

---

23 Pew Forum, 'The Future of the Global Muslim Population', 2011. http://www.pewforum .org/2011/01/27/future-of-the-global-muslim-population-regional-europe/#4. Accessed 23 December 2014.

24 Adrian Michaels, 'A fifth of European Union will be Muslim by 2050', *The Telegraph*, August 2009. <http://www.telegraph.co.uk/news/worldnews/europe/5994045/A-fifth-of -European-Union-will-be-Muslim-by-2005.html> accessed 23 Dec 2014.

25 Read more at http://www.wnd.com/2006/05/35992/#m6VskrUgZWkX73rp.99. Accessed 27 Dec 2014.

A certain segment of the population doesn't want to hear this news. So we find responses like, "No, Muslims are not taking over the world," the title of an article in *The Guardian*, a mouthpiece for secular multiculturalism.[26] In this article we are informed that all the worry is overblown because "the global Muslim population is projected to grow at a slower pace than it did during the previous two decades." But why does that matter? What matters is that the worldwide Muslim population is in fact still growing quickly, while European populations are declining and will continue to do so, and a steady ingress of Muslim migrants to Europe will certainly continue to take place with no sign of letting up. Those are the issues when it comes to Europe. The title of the article is also deceptive, because it implies that people concerned about the growth of Islam (in the West, particularly) are wild-eyed fanatics who are intolerant. The preachy article, co-authored by John Esposito, the founding director of Prince Alwaleed Center for Muslim-Christian Understanding,[27] concludes:

> The reality is that there is no takeover, but that there is a danger of intolerance that threatens the very fabric of British and European society. We are not witnessing a clash of civilisations, but a clash of cultures fostered by those who portray Islam as a monolith and see religious and cultural diversity solely as a threat rather than as a potential source of strength and enrichment.

I will soon address the sophistry of the "monolith fallacy," but first let us return to my initial hypothesis: that Muslims will be the plurality in most urban centers of Western Europe by 2100. If that does take place, and I think it is the most reasonable outcome of the migration and fertility realities outlined here, then we can expect for Europe to change. Logically, it will look more like the societies of its new inhabitants and the

---

26 http://www.theguardian.com/commentisfree/belief/2011/feb/11/islam-population.
Accessed 23 Dec 2014.

27 Prince Alwaleed is of the royal house of Saud, which rules over Saudi Arabia. That Esposito's position and income are related to the wealth of this prince has come under criticism, leading to him being charged as being an "apologist for Wahhabi Islam" (see http://www.americanthinker.com/articles/2011/09/john_l_esposito_apologist_for_ wahhabi_islam.html). Saudi Arabia is one of the most intolerant countries in the entire world in terms of religious freedom.

children and grandchildren of such immigrants. Furthermore, the naïve assumption that Muslims (and others) will blindly assimilate ignores two realities: first, that the Islamic metanarrative is much more compelling and vigorous than the bankrupt, vacuous, materialistic metanarrative of secular humanism; and second, that it is not always the case that the second or third generation will be 'more' European than the first generation of immigrants. July 7 is a reminder of this. It was on that day in 2005 that a number of British-born, middle class Muslims exploded four bombs targeting the transportation systems of London, resulting in over 50 deaths and hundreds of injuries. These young men were brought up in the UK and received all the benefits of living in that society.

Indeed, as European identity continues to become more and more detached from its roots in Christendom, one must ask, why should the Muslim immigrant respect 'British' values or 'German' values? What is their origin? A historically informed answer would list the three primary contributors to Western civilization: Germanic heritage, Greco-Roman heritage, and Judeo-Christian heritage. But to acknowledge this is to acknowledge that Europe is founded on the Christian faith to a substantial degree. But it is anathema today to acknowledge this simple historical reality. So the immigrant is left asking, "If your laws and morality are not in some way based on the will of the Creator of the universe, and it is true that no one culture is superior to any other (the heart of multiculturalism), then why should I respect you culture and morality, much less cherish them?"

One response to the immigrant's question is this: These are the values that made the UK prosperous and educated, unlike your own home country of Pakistan (for instance). You enjoy the prosperity and freedoms afforded to you in the UK (for instance), and so you should appreciate and abide by our legal and moral systems. But such discourse is likely to meet with charges of racism, Islamophobia, or intolerance. This is because the logical implication of such an argument is that British culture is superior to the culture and morality of Pakistan. Furthermore, there is a general consensus among the elite (including academics) that whatever problems may exist in countries like Pakistan must be the fault of the West. In our hypothetical example, the endemic nepotism and corruption of Pakistani politics might be blamed entirely on the trauma of the post-colonial experience, and one will have no trouble finding numerous academics to support this position.

What will Europe look like in 2100 then? It will probably look like any other part of the world with Muslim pluralities in the centers of power. It is true that many Muslims are indeed happy to be apolitical and have a "live and let live" attitude. This is true for most Christians as well. But wherever you have a substantial population of Muslims (especially a plurality) you will, by the very dynamic of the metanarrative of Islam, have zealous and energetic people. These people, in their devotion to God and his benevolent will for humanity (the shari'a), will organize and deploy their resources, wealth, and numbers to modify or subvert the existing laws. As a consequence, the local laws will more and more be influenced by the shari'a or allow for the shari'a to take over parts of the civil law (like banking or family law). This is not part of some nefarious plot. Rather, a Muslim might look at life in the UK and think, this is much better than it was in Pakistan, but wouldn't it be even better (especially for Muslims, the best of all peoples) if this were a shari'a state?

The important thing for Christians to remember is that Europe *is not* the faith, nor is the faith Europe. As much as Christianity's history appears to be intertwined with that of Europe, its story is in fact much larger than the history of Europe. Christianity has lost great centers of the faith before—places like Carthage, Edessa, Alexandria, and Constantinople. But does this mean that the *umma* is accomplishing its calling from Allah? I think that, in spite of the apparent (demographic and migratory) success of Islam in Europe we need to ask some harder questions. Is that all there is to Islam? To have political control? That strikes me as a fairly shallow reading of Allah's purpose for the *umma*.

Shari'a is supposed to *work*. That is, it is supposed to lead to a prosperous, just society. But where is it actually working in the world today? One can find Islamic countries that are not terrible failures—many cite Turkey, Malaysia, and Indonesia (though all three countries are becoming less tolerant, not more tolerant). The relative success of Turkey is *not* related to the shari'a—on the contrary, the secular government (which is becoming more and more Islamized) founded by Kemal Ataturk was explicitly organized in order to *eschew* a shari'a state. Indeed, it was as part of this project of secularization that the Istanbul-based caliphate was dissolved in 1924!

In any case, given that there are several dozen countries with various forms of the shari'a, one would expect this to be working in at least a few of them. But where are the success stories? Where exactly is Islam working? When we look at the shari'a in action, in many ways it resembles Communism in the 50s and 60s. Communists were sure that it would work and that it would lead to the workers' paradise. But when asked about the various communist countries, they would say, "Well, it works, it is just not being applied *there*"—East Germany, China, Romania, etc.

One common response I have heard from Muslims to the unseemly reality that (excepting sub-Saharan Africa) Muslim countries are regularly among the worst performers in the world when it comes to human rights, education, and economic growth, is that Islamic countries really can't thrive due to a huge, multinational plot of Zionists and Crusaders who intentionally are holding down Islam; it is not the fault of the shari'a or the *umma*. They would say that the Zionists and Crusaders accomplish this in various ways, like propping up the tyrannical governments of certain dictators, or invading and occupying Muslims lands. In other words, this strategy views Muslims as the global victims, sometimes of other Muslims such as the House of Saud or the Al Asad regime in Syria. Ultimately, though, Muslims are victims of the West and Israel. In my experience, a strong conviction that Muslims are the victims par excellence of the entire world is very common.

Perhaps an example will help: Once I was talking with a cab driver in an Arab country, and he was complaining about world politics. I, somewhat exasperated, observed, "You know what the problem here is? You don't have any men—just boys." He asked me to explain myself. "A man," I said, "will look around and realize that he has some problems, some of them he can work on and make better, others maybe he can't do anything about. A man will tackle the problems he can, but a little boy will just whine about not getting his way. This country has no men." I was not trying to be mean in saying this, and I was surprised to see him nodding before he said, "You're right."

I am talking about a tendency here, not a rule. Indeed, every now and then you will find an article in a magazine or local newspaper that says our poor educational system (for instance) is our own fault—stop blaming America and Israel. But for every article like this, you will have ten more complaining about the perpetual victimhood of Muslims. Let me also note here that this sense of perpetual and universal victimhood is related to the topic of jihad, because if you are always and everywhere a victim, then any act of violence you carry out is *ipso facto* an act of self-defense, and even outside of Islam most everyone agrees that a defensive war is just—just as self-defense was an initial justification for the Crusades.

The logic of victimhood explains everything—there is no possible piece of evidence that can count against it. Consider: in the 1990s when the USA and the West left Saddam Hussein in power, refusing to occupy Iraq, and used economic sanctions against the Hussein regime, they were accused of harming the poor, normal Iraqis. When the USA supported Egyptian president Hosni Mubarak in the 1990s and early 2000s, it was guilty of colluding with a tyrant. When the USA actually invaded Iraq in 2003 to unseat Hussein and the Ba'th regime, the motive was obviously to despoil the oil wealth of the Iraqi people. Examples of this can be provided ad infinitum. No matter what happens in the world, there is some way to construe it as one step in a huge plot aimed at subverting the success of the *umma*. The West has no way to win in the Middle East when it comes to foreign policy, just many different ways to lose, all of which end up with the West as bad guy and the Muslim the powerless victim.

This is the opposite of what you often find among the intelligentsia of Europe and America. Many have a strong tendency to view any problem in the world as the fault of the West. At least Muslims have the conviction that their *umma* is *good* and part of God's plan—it is just being held down by the (Zionist-Crusader) man.

It is not a very empowering vision, is it? This is why I often quote the Qur'anic verse, "Allah does not change the lot of a people until they change what is in themselves."[28] I like this verse because (unlike many other verses in the Qur'an) it emphasizes something we call agency, which is the use of power to achieve the interests of a society. Muslims can improve their circumstances, and we should encourage *some* groups that are trying to do this. Of course, other groups that are trying to do this are labeled as terrorist.

---

28   13:11

There is a problem with placing the blame for shari'a not working on thinking that the *umma* is being held down by the Zionist-Crusader plot. First, any political system must be able to recognize that there will always be those who oppose it, both from within and without. If the shari'a does not have a workable way to address this issue, then it *doesn't* work. In other words, even if there were a secret plot to undermine Islam, a revealed, divine political system should certainly be able to address and subvert such a plot and emerge victorious. Perhaps that is what Gadhafi was pointing to above—that once Islam has become victorious over Europe (by migration and fertility, not bombs and wars), *then* the plot will have been undermined and the *umma* will be able to spread its wings, and we will (finally) see the just and triumphant Islamic society that has been so widely advertised.

Some Muslims have realized this and, exercising agency, have taken matters into their own hands. This is certainly part of the impetus behind the rise of the Islamic State: "Pure shari'a is not being applied and executed by any of the so-called 'Islamic states' in the world." Therefore they found it necessary to create a new state. Indeed, it is not only *a* new Islamic state, but is *the* Islamic State, with a caliph and everything.

So how is the *umma* doing in its divine mission of spreading the divine shari'a all over the world? I would give it a D, meaning that the *umma* is largely failing. The reality that there are so many shari'a states today that, in all their variety, are not delivering on the promises of Islam is a sign of this failure. However, there are authentic and genuine attempts to change this—some militant and violent, others intellectual and peaceful— and these movements are the one thing keeping the community of Islamic metanarrative from getting an F—which is to say *completely* failing. That Europe will likely become predominantly Islamic in many of its urban centers by 2100 will give Muslims fertile new ground to test their visions of what a shari'a state should look like. Furthermore, the Islamic State, as controversial as it is, is also a novel and creative attempt to address the apparent failure of shari'a around the world.

One more word on Islam in Europe. I had pointed out above what I call the "monolith fallacy," and I wish to explore this briefly here, for it is common in academia and the media: Whenever anyone says something about Muslims in Europe they say, "Yes, but aren't you essentializing Islam and treating Muslims as a monolithic group?" This all sounds very intelligent and enlightened. What does it mean? Essentialize means to "reduce to essentials" according to Merriam-Webster. The other fancy word here is "monolithic." A *monolith* is a very large stone that is usually tall and erect. The adjective here means "constituting a massive undifferentiated and often rigid whole" (Merriam-Webster again). The valid kernel at the heart of this observation is that there is a great deal of variety among Muslims. I know this and repeatedly have stated it. Indeed, the progressives and multiculturalists who insist (with Obama and Cameron and Bush) that militant reformist Islam (like Al Qaeda and the Islamic State) is not "real Islam" are in fact ignoring this reality. Surely not all Muslims are like that, but that some are (probably *not* a tiny minority), is plain to see.

But in the hand of some academics and the elite, this line of thinking is often used to close off all critical discussion of Islam. Here is the trick: It is true that Islam is not "monolithic" and there is a great deal of variety among Muslims. Therefore, not all Muslims support violence or the subversion of Western values. Therefore, shut up and don't talk about the people who *do* want to subvert Western values. But I respond: according to the metanarrative of Islam, which has been outlined here, sooner or later *some* Muslims *must* try to establish political control or influence, because they need the power of law to enjoin what is right and forbid what is wrong (Qur'an 3:104)—this is the whole purpose of the *umma* and, moreover, it is Allah's will. That was the great success of Muhammad, after all, when he went from merely having a religious message (in Mecca) to obtaining legal and military power whereby he could obtain a monopoly on coercion. This he did upon the hijra to Yathrib, which is the beginning of the Islamic calendar.

Think of it like this: if you have the Christian faith taking root in a society that previously had no Christians, you will first see churches. Some will be home churches, but eventually the demands of the community will grow and you will probably have structures (church buildings) devoted to the worship and life of that community. As it grows, the community will not be monolithic: some will be more devout, others less; some more conservative, others less; some wanting to center the religious identity on the local, others on the universal. As the number of Christians grows, one would not be surprised to see certain sodalities arise. Sodalities are like guilds or associations that are attached to the Church but not congregations in and of themselves. They might be a religious order like the Franciscans or a society founded for a particular purpose, like a Christian school, a clinic, a student association, a prison ministry, a missionary society, a seminary, etc. As the number of Christians grows, one would not be surprised to see these sodalities arise. Nor are *all* Christians part of those sodalities, nor is membership in a sodality a requisite for belonging to the overarching modality of the Church.[29]

My point is that sodalities or groups within the larger *umma* that seek to obtain legal or extralegal power to enjoin what is good and forbid what is wrong *must* arise sooner or later as a Muslim population grows in a given place. Some such sodalities work within the structures of the state (or university or prison), others work outside of them knowing that the existing pagan laws are not, in fact, real laws at all, because all authentic law emanates from God himself. Any "law" that limits the ability of the *umma* to carry out its mission is, *ipso facto*, null and void. Not all Muslims think along these lines, but some do. How many? No one knows because the people who believe thus will, for obvious reasons, rarely publicly disclose it.

The only person who could be surprised by this is a person who is ignorant of the metanarrative of Islam. That the West as a whole has failed to grasp this reality is clear by its persistent misclassification of Islam as "a religion" *simpliciter*. In sum, not all Muslims in a community will be directly devoted to the accumulation of political power—and violence against those who demur—in order to assist the *umma* in its divine mission of enjoining the right and forbidding the wrong, but some will. Indeed, the Islamic metanarrative requires it once the *umma*'s presence makes this possible. This is a reasoned response to *the monolith fallacy*.

Why secular (atheistic) humanism will fail

At this point, let's take a brief look at a third metanarrative—that of secular (and often atheistic) humanism. Secular humanism, the religion of

---

29 For more on the missionary dynamic of the modality/sodality nature of the Church see Ralph Winters' "The Two Structures of God's Redemptive Missions" (http://frontiermissionfellowship.org/uploads/documents/two-structures.pdf)

most contemporary atheists, has its own articles of faith, anthropology, and creation myths. It places the individual human at the center of the universe and allows, or even insists, that this human construct her own system of identity, value, and axiology—what Peter Berger calls the *heretical imperative*.[30] After the so-called Enlightenment many assumed that "objective reason" would be triumphant. Religion, based on faith (which is essentially irrational and subjective), would die out. But a funny thing happened on the way to the 21st Century, and today, apart from pockets of North America and Western Europe, the world as a whole is growing more religious, not less so. As Rodney Stark, distinguished professor of social sciences at Baylor University, recently noted, "It is a very religious world, far more religious than it was 50 years ago."[31]

The collapse of the Soviet Union in 1990 is one piece of this puzzle. The decline of Pan-Arab nationalism (which tended to be nationalist and more secular) is evident in the failure of the experiment of the United Arab Republic (1961). Also, two of the main secular Arab countries—Iraq and Syria—are no longer secular and, one might argue, are no longer coherent nation states. The explosive growth of Pentecostalism in Africa and Latin America, the rise of Hindu nationalism in India, the growth of Christianity in China, the emergence of new religious movements[32] all around the world—these are all other pieces in this puzzle, revealing how religion is becoming more influential globally, and not less so. And even Europe, often held up as a paragon of non-religion, does not necessarily fit into the atheistic future:

> Attendance at Europe's very limited variety of Christian churches is very low. Even so, most Europeans still hold religious beliefs and atheists are few—an average of 6.6 percent in Western Europe and 4.6 percent in the East. And, as is typical where conventional religion is weak, unconventional and unorganized "faiths" abound in the vacuum.

---

30 *Heretical Imperative* (Doubleday, 1980). See also the book edited by him, *The Desecularization of the World* (Eerdmans, 1999).

31 "A Worldwide Religious Awakening," www.slate.com/bigideas/what-is-the-future-of-religion/essays-and-opinions/rodney-stark-opinion, accessed 7 Jan 2015.

32 This is the term in academia, but in common parlance many of these communities would be called cults.

Occult movements are rife. So is belief in fortune-tellers, astrology, lucky charms, and psychic healers. Spiritualism is popular, especially in the Nordic nations, and many dabble in all manner of New Age activities. So much for claims that Europeans have "outgrown" belief in the supernatural.[33]

Nonetheless, we still find arguments that the world as a whole is moving away from religion. The argument goes like this: every society that becomes more modern and prosperous becomes less religious (and importantly, less fertile). As the world becomes more prosperous and developed, people worldwide will become less religious and fertile. Similarly, as Muslims continue to migrate to Europe, they too will become less fertile and less religious.

Do you see the errors? It is true that countries do indeed tend to lower fertility and increase disaffiliation (not belonging to any specific religious community) as they become more prosperous. Many of the things that attract people to religion, like prayers for healing or pastoral guidance, have substitutes in medical care and psychology. Many of the traditional roles of the church and mosque, like taking care of orphans, the elderly, and the sick, and providing education are now provided by the state, further marginalizing those institutions. Furthermore, the basis of human rights is dislocated from being made in God's image (a Judeo-Christian doctrine) to an arbitrary and indefensible theory that assigns the label of "human right" to whatever happens to be *en vogue* at the moment among the liberal intelligentsia.

If one is looking ten or twenty years down the road then it is likely that secular humanism will continue to grow in a few societies: the USA, Canada, Western Europe, Australia, and Japan. But it is an irrational leap to conclude from this that it will spread to the rest of the world. After all, what is the basis for assuming that the rest of the world is going to become like Europe? Remember that the indigenous populations of all of these countries are at or below replacement fertility. Nigel Barber, author of *Why Atheism will Replace Religion*, summarizes his argument in an article for the Huffington Post, and concludes that "religion (however measured)

---

33   Rodney Stark, "Religious Awakening", NP.

is in sharp decline in the most developed countries that enjoy the highest standard of living for most of the people, namely social democracies such as Japan and Sweden."[34]

Japan, for one, is already in a state of population decline. Sweden is often trotted out as a success story, showing how a country can be both secular *and* avoid ultra-low fertility. The TFR of Sweden is 1.9, which is closer to replacement than most Western European countries. But is Sweden really a success story? I don't think so, at least not over the long term. First, the TFR of Sweden *is* below replacement. Second, foreign-born women in Sweden (not all of whom are Muslims) have a higher fertility (2.21) than do Swedish-born women (1.88).[35] Meanwhile, Sweden welcomes refugees and migrants in substantial numbers, with Iraq, Iran, Somalia, and Turkey having significant migrant communities, and with Syria, Somalia, Afghanistan, Eritrea and Iran being main sources of new migrants between 2012 and 2013. The summers of 2015 and 2016 have witnessed an enormous migration of Syrians—almost all Muslims—to Sweden and Germany. Moreover, recently this has led to flare-ups in violence against Muslim immigrants.[36] In sum, Sweden has a quickly growing Muslim population; non-Swedish women have more children than Swedish women; Swedish women reproduce *below* replacement rate. All of this in spite of the fact that Sweden has one of the highest fertility rates in Europe.

Rather than imagining that prosperity, and with it secularism/atheism, is going to spread, it is more reasonable to project that the prosperity of Europe will decline. What is it that makes a society prosperous? As Daren Acemoglu and James A. Robinson argue in *Why Nations Fail: The Origins of Power, Prosperity, and Poverty*,[37] a foundation for prosperity is the existence of inclusive institutions. Just because you move a population (such as Iraqis, Syrians, or Somalis) to a country that has these prosperity-creating inclusive institutions does not necessarily mean that these new

---

34   "Can Atheism Really Replace Religion?" in *Huffington Post* (www.huffingtonpost.com/nigel-barber/can-atheism-really-replace-religion_b_3355172.html, accessed 31 December 2014).

35   David Landes, "Higher birth rates among Sweden's foreign-born" in *The Local* (Nov 2008), at www.thelocal.se/20081103/15408, accessed 31 Dec 2014.

36   Stephen Castle, "Tension Over Swedish Immigration Rises . . ." in *The New York Times* (Dec 2014) (nyti.ms/1BbhWZt, accessed 31 Dec 2015)

37   Crown, 2012.

populations will join and/or perpetuate those institutions. Indeed, it is not reasonable to assume that immigrant populations will do so, nor do I see substantial evidence that this is taking place. Why do we think that the nepotism so common in Arab society will be replaced by the more European meritocracy? Or why do we think that the patronage systems known to Muslims will be discarded in order to perpetuate the socialist democratic system of Sweden—unless of course they will profit from it?

Here is an example from Sweden: the country is a champion of women's rights, yet Sweden is, after the tiny African country of Lesotho, the rape capital of the world:

> In 1975, the Swedish parliament unanimously decided to change the former homogeneous Sweden into a multicultural country. Forty years later the dramatic consequences of this experiment emerge: violent crime has increased by 300%.
>
> If one looks at the number of rapes, however, the increase is even worse. In 1975, 421 rapes were reported to the police; in 2014, it was 6,620. That is an increase of 1,472%.
>
> Sweden is now number two on the global list of rape countries. According to a survey from 2010, Sweden, with 53.2 rapes per 100,000 inhabitants . . .[38]

Michael Hess, a Swedish politician, stated that, "There is a strong connection between rapes in Sweden and the number of immigrants from MENA-countries [Middle East and North Africa]." For this he was charged with the crime of denigrating an ethnic group.

> As part of the evidence Michael Hess presented in court, he made use of whatever statistics existed on immigrant criminality in Sweden before the statistical authorities stopped measuring. Michael Hess tried to find answers to two questions:
>
> Is there a correspondence between the incidence of rape and the number of people with a foreign background in Sweden?

---

38   Ingrid Carlqvist and Lars Hedegaard, "Sweden: Rape Capital of the West", February 14, 2015. http://www.gatestoneinstitute.org/5195/sweden-rape

Is there a correspondence between the incidence of rape and some specific group of immigrants in Sweden?

The answer to both questions was an unequivocal Yes. Twenty-one research reports from the 1960s until today are unanimous in their conclusions: Whether or not they measured by the number of convicted rapists or men suspected of rape, men of foreign extraction were represented far more than Swedes. And this greater representation of persons with a foreign background keeps increasing:

1960-1970s – 1.2 to 2.6 times as often as Swedes
1980s – 2.1 to 4.7 times as often as Swedes
1990s – 2.1 to 8.1 times as often as Swedes
2000s – 2.1 to 19.5 times as often as Swedes

Even when adjusted for variables such as age, sex, class and place of residence, the huge discrepancy between immigrants and Swedes remains.[39]

The Swedish cultural institution of egalitarianism and women's rights has not been adopted by a substantial number of its immigrants. What surprises me is that anyone is surprised by this.

This is an error that many people make: to suppose that just because a population will receive the benefits of Western institutions that they actually like them, support them, or believe them to be good. I think that relatively few people go to Europe and North America because they understand, much less love, the vision, history, and tradition of those countries. Nor, indeed, are the countries in those areas particularly proud of their institutions and practices that have helped to create prosperous societies. People migrate to Europe and North America to receive the *benefits* of those institutions and practices—not to perpetuate and foster them. Immigrating to the West does not necessarily lead to people adopting the metanarrative of the West. One of the main insights to be gained from Niall Ferguson's brilliant *Civilization: The West and the Rest*,[40] is that the traditions and institutions (Ferguson calls them *killer apps*) of the West that led to its great success are now being discarded *by* the West.

---

39   *ibid.*
40   Penguin, 2012

Furthermore, it is well known that religiosity (how often one attends their church, synagogue, mosque, or temple) is positively correlated to fertility.[41] That is, women who practice their religions have more children. For the West, this is true regardless of whether we are speaking of Muslims, Christians, or Jews. Because of this, I do think that a relatively small but vibrant community of practicing, devout Christians will continue to be present in most European cities. Christianity will look more and more African as the decades progress, as I mentioned above.

The result of all of this is that as we continue to approach 2100 we will see a small and dwindling *secular* ethnic European population and growing Muslim populations. The institutions of those Islamic communities will have been preserved and even protected because of Europe's commitment to multiculturalism, which insists that European institutions and practices are *not* superior to those of the immigrants' native communities.

But is it not possible to inform or order immigrants to learn the institutions and customs of the secular Europeans, under the rubric of "British values" or "Danish values"? It may be possible to compel immigrants to gain a basic historical and cultural knowledge of the European country, but it is not possible to compel them to ascribe any value to that history and culture. Furthermore, telling people they can live in Europe but must substantially *discard* their own institutions and practices and adopt those of Europe would likely be ruled a violation of the (arbitrary) human rights of those communities by the European Court of Human Rights. Because of this, the set of institutions and practices that created a prosperous Europe will not spread to other parts of the world.[42] On the contrary, those institutions in Europe will, I suspect, decline and deteriorate along with the shrinking, secular-atheist populations whose (Christian) ancestors created and fostered them. London will become more like Lahore and Belgium like Morocco and Germany like Turkey—not the other way around.

---

41   For instance, see Tanya Lewis, "Baby Boom: Religious Women Having More Kids" in *LiveScience* (Aug 2013) at http://www.livescience.com/38743-religious-women-having-more-babies.html, accessed 31 Dec 2014.

42   I am intentional in referring to the *set* of institutions and practices. Countries may adopt one or two of these institutions, as China has adopted the so-called Protestant work ethic and aspects of capitalism, while not adopting other institutions, like rule of law.

In sum, I do not find an atheistic/secular future in the cards for Europe, Canada, or Australia.[43] Atheists do not have enough children to make that happen, and the prosperity that leads to secularism will likewise deteriorate because of migration, fertility, and the fact that prosperity-creating institutions will decline with the populations who historically founded them. They will be substantially and gradually replaced or reshaped by the institutions and practices that failed to produce prosperity and/or stability in the home countries of Europe's new citizens.

Conclusion

The Church, as a percentage of the world population, has not grown significantly between 1900 and 2000. The *umma*, on the contrary, has grown significantly. Growth is to be expected in a healthy community. Few people would look at Japan or Russia with their shrinking populations and think they are healthy; no one would look at a company losing market share and think that is good. In the same way, the dramatic growth of a religious community like the *umma* is striking and most Muslims evaluate this positively. Growth is often a sign of health. However, neither the Church nor the *umma* were founded *solely* for the sake of being big. The Church, if it is a body of disciples making other disciples, and indeed crossing geographical, social, cultural, and ethnic boundaries in order to make those disciples (that is the *go* in the Great Commission), then one would reasonably expect the Church to be a growing body. Similarly, the *umma* has a divine mission to see that all humanity lives according to God's will, the shari'a. Yes, sometimes that does mean fighting—and why do people think this is not logical?—Muhammad himself said, in his final sermon, "I was ordered to fight all men until they say, 'There is no god but

---

43   The USA is difficult to understand here. Its population is more religious and fertile (though that is decreasing) than that of Europe. Also, a relatively small percentage of its immigrants are Muslims. I do think the central point holds though, that as the USA becomes more Latino, the institutions and practices of the USA will increasingly resemble those of Latin America. Of course the predominant metanarratives of Latin America— Christianity and Secular Humanism—are the predominant metanarratives in the USA.

Allah.'"[44] As people see the attractive society of the *umma* they should logically desire to enter and live according to it.

In spite of the lackluster performance of the Church in making disciples of *all peoples* and the less-than-stellar performance of the *umma* in establishing and living according to the shari'a, there are pockets of activity here and there. In terms of taking the Gospel to the unreached peoples of the world, almost all progress was made by evangelical/pentecostal Christians. Regarding the *umma*, we don't find a resounding example of success, but there has been no lack of trying—I think here of the vanguard of the Muslim Brotherhood, reform movements like Al Qaeda, and the Islamic State.

Muslim pluralities, non-monolithic though they may be, will continue to consolidate in major European urban centers in the 21st Century. They will increasingly experiment with different approaches to grafting features of the shari'a into existing civil codes—examples are the increased use of shari'a contracts for loans and family law—and this is already taking place. This will offer the world additional opportunities to see the *umma* in action.

Discussion Questions

What is the significance of abrogation?

What is the relation between abrogation and the common characterization of Islam as "a religion of peace"?

Is there another word other than "religion" that can be used to describe Islam?

The author argues that there is a strong sense of victimhood among many Muslims today. Why is this important? Does this strike you as accurate or not? What would a Christian response to this reality look like?

What do you think about the author's argument and evidence for an irreversible decline of secular humanism in the form of Western civilization?

---

44   Quoted in Ephraim Karsh's *Islamic Imperialism* (Yale University Press, 2006), p 1.

Eight

ESCHATOLOGY

Eschatology means *the study of last things.* These last things include the final events in human history, God's final and radical intervention into this world, and the eternal destiny of human souls. Eschatology answers the question: how does the story end?

This is also the part of the book I most did not want to write. The reason for this is simple: it is very sloppy—especially for Christians. You can make certain broad generalizations about Holy Communion or the atonement and feel relatively confident that most orthodox Christian will agree with you. That is much harder to do with eschatology because there is more than one way of reading and interpreting various prophetic texts in the Bible. For instance, many evangelical Christians read Revelation as depicting events that still lie largely in the future. Furthermore, it is not clear what language in Revelation is figurative and what is not figurative.[1] There are, however, other very profitable ways of reading the book of Revelation (as well as other prophetic texts) that have their own integrity, but which are not understood as laying out a detailed map of the future.

---

1   It is common to hear people talking about reading the Bible "literally." I intentionally avoid such language because the way people use the word is incorrect. The next time you hear someone use the word, ask them exactly what they mean; it is unlikely they will be able to precisely define the term. Even liberals take the Bible literally where the Bible says Jesus was crucified under Pilate; even fundamentalists take the Bible figuratively when the Bible says, "God is a rock."

This is not an argument about liberal or modernist interpretations of Scripture. As I have outlined before, I am specifically trying to stay away from what Muslims call *bid'a* or innovation (a serious sin in Islam, and an insight I am sympathetic towards). Modern revisionist interpretations of Scripture have no future because they belong to dying churches that, like ethnic Europeans, lack the fecundity to reproduce each generation with another generation of equal or greater size. The fruitful Christians who make disciples of their own children will certainly have a church home in the future, just not in those declining denominations.

With these limitations in mind, let us proceed.

Commonalities

There are, in fact, many commonalities between Muslims and Christians in terms of how their Scriptures describe the end days. Both predict a large-scale falling away from the faith before the end, involve the bodily return of Jesus Christ, envision divine celestial portents, speak of the rise of a deceitful anti-Christ figure, an apocalyptic battle in Greater Syria, and the great and final judgment of every human soul from Adam forward in the context of a resurrection of all of humanity. Finally, for the blessed, both metanarratives end with eternal felicity in a paradise, and for the damned with eternal suffering in fire.

Why so much commonality? Perhaps because both metanarratives grew out of the soil of Jewish apocalyptic literature, but the specific roots are not of particular import to us. What *is* of import is to trace and suggest how the eschatological visions of the two metanarratives wrap up or conclude the two different central problems in each of these two metanarratives.

Christianity

Jesus himself had a good deal to say about the end, or, as the Hebrew prophets called it, the Day of the Lord. Several of his parables talk about the final judgment, including the parable of the net, the parable of the wheat and tares, and the parable of the goats and the sheep. He affirmed a universal and final judgment, and in John's Gospel went so far as to affirm that he himself in his body was actually the resurrection (John 11:25). Matthew, Mark, and Luke all have him presenting an apocalyptic sermon known as the Olivet Discourse during Holy Week. During this sermon he talks about the destruction of the Jerusalem Temple and what the world will look like prior to his second coming (paraousia is the technical term). The details include wars among the nations, signs in the heavens, false prophets, and the persecution of Jesus' disciples. It is important to note that Jesus ties these apocalyptic events to the completion of the Church's missio ad gentes: "And the gospel must first be proclaimed to all nations." (Mark 13:10).

Paradoxically, the persecution of Christians and the rise of violence and war are tied to the Church's fulfillment of her *telos* (object, end, or aim)—to go into the world and make disciples of *all* peoples. Revelation, the final book of the Bible, envisions what this fulfillment will look like in the words of a hymn of praise to Jesus the Lamb of God: "Worthy are you to take the scroll and to open its seals, for you were slain, and by your blood you ransomed people for God from every tribe and language and people and nation, and you have made them a kingdom and priests to our God, and they shall reign on the earth" (Revelation 5:9b, 10).

And it is precisely the *telos* and mission of the Church to announce the Gospel throughout the whole earth so that people will have the option to accept this invitation to be cleansed by the blood of the Lamb and incorporated into this Kingdom of God—the very Kingdom of which Jesus taught so often. Once the Church is done with its work, and God gathers for himself a group of worshipers from every tribe and tongue and nation, *then* the end will come.

The Christian metanarrative envisions the personal and bodily return of Jesus Christ to the earth. Scripture uses personification to describe how even the very physical material of the Creation is yearning for this day (Romans 8:19). This is well within our metanarrative because we saw that at the entry of death into Creation even nature itself became alienated from God. The new creation that was begun in Jesus' resurrected body will not only spread to the resurrection of all the saved, but even to the natural order which will be "a new heaven and a new earth" (Rev. 21:1). I do not read this as the total destruction of the present Creation, but rather the present Creation, like Jesus' body, being glorified, or perhaps renewed, just as our bodies will be renewed.

Revelation 21:1-8 (whether you read it figuratively or as an actual and physical historical event that will take place) gives us some good hints as to what this New Creation will be like:

> Then I saw a new heaven and a new earth, for the first heaven and the first earth had passed away, and the sea was no more. And I saw the holy city, new Jerusalem, coming down out of heaven from God, prepared as a bride adorned for her husband. And I heard a loud voice from the throne saying, "Behold, the dwelling place of God is with man. He will dwell with them, and they will be his people, and God himself will be with them as their God. He will wipe away every tear from their eyes, and death shall be no more, neither shall there be mourning, nor crying, nor pain anymore, for the former things have passed away."
>
> And he who was seated on the throne said, "Behold, I am making all things new." Also he said, "Write this down, for these words are trustworthy and true." And he said to me, "It is done! I am the Alpha and the Omega, the beginning and the end. To the thirsty I will give from the spring of the water of life without payment. The one who conquers will have this heritage, and I will be his God and he will be my son. But as for the cowardly, the faithless, the detestable, as for murderers, the sexually immoral, sorcerers, idolaters, and all liars, their portion will be in the lake that burns with fire and sulfur, which is the second death."

As mentioned above, the Creation is not so much a different one as a new, glorified one, or as Jesus says, "Behold, I am making all things new."[2] This is the renewal of which I just spoke.

---

2 There is a beautiful Greek word for this reconstitution or restoration of the cosmos, *apocatastasis*. It appears a single time in the New Testament: "Repent therefore, and turn back, that your sins may be blotted out, that times of refreshing may come from the presence of the Lord, and that he may send the Christ appointed for you, Jesus, whom heaven must receive until the time for *restoring all the things* about which God spoke by the mouth of his holy prophets long ago" (Acts 3:19-21).

We also see that the eternal future of the saved is not floating with God in heaven, but that God's heavenly city is merged with earth. The Kingdom of God which Jesus had announced is now *here* in its totality. The city of God descending and then being in the midst of humanity and inhabited by humanity represents the conclusion of Jesus' ministry. This is also seen in how the final enemy, death, is overcome (v. 14). The conviction that death is the ultimate enemy is also found in 1 Corinthians 15:20-26, where Paul ties Jesus' resurrection to the eschatological victory over death:

> But in fact Christ has been raised from the dead, the firstfruits of those who have fallen asleep. For as by a man came death, by a man has come also the resurrection of the dead. For as in Adam all die, so also in Christ shall all be made alive. But each in his own order: Christ the firstfruits, then at his coming those who belong to Christ. Then comes the end, when he delivers the kingdom to God the Father after destroying every rule and every authority and power. For he must reign until he has put all his enemies under his feet. The last enemy to be destroyed is death.

Finally, the new Creation and the resurrection signify the conclusion of salvation. That is, it is at this point that people will be able to say, "I have been saved" rather than "I am being saved."

But what of damnation? This is not a very comfortable Christian teaching for most people today. It doesn't seem to square with a loving God in the American mind. The belief in eternal damnation, however, is an authentic feature of historical Christian doctrine. It is clear that Jesus taught about it and throughout history it has often been those people who are holiest and most filled with God's love who are the most aware of the reality of hell. Revelation 21 presents us with the image of a lake of fire, though there are other biblical images for hell as well, like the Valley of Hinnom (Gehenna) or the outer darkness (The image of Gehenna is used in the Qur'an over 70 times in reference to damnation).

In Revelation 21 the Lake of Fire is not prepared for humans. Rather, it is prepared for the devil and his angels. But it is out of respect for the reality of human free will that God must allow for some strange sort of existence for the souls of those who opted to be their own gods during their lifetimes.

The name for this sin is idolatry, and as much as it represents a defiling of God and a repudiation of our just duty owed to him as our Creator, it is primarily a degradation and abasement of the self. With this truth in mind we are able to grasp why the sin of idolatry is the concern of the first two of the Ten Commandments. In the end the human soul can worship and serve its Creator, or it can worship and serve itself, making it to be its own god. And each soul will spend eternity with its god. The God of the Bible is not coercive in that way—he will not force souls that have freely opted to worship themselves and be their own idols to spend an eternity with him.

The image of the ultimate solitude and loneliness of a soul alone for eternity with its own god (its self) comes across well in the symbol of the outer darkness. Jesus himself is the light of the world, his community must be light, and the psalms use luminous metaphors for God ("a sun and shield" Psalm 84:11). Ultimately reason is not light, but God, who is in himself truth, is light. Separated from God the soul decays. Reason paired with humility leads to that Light; reason that overestimates its power becomes an idol. Darkness then is the absence of this light, and an outer darkness implies being very distant or completely separated from any light at all.

I have been teaching undergrads long enough to be familiar with some of their rejoinders. Many are serious and searching, but at times one hears, only half in jest, that it is better to party in hell with the sinners than to weep (or reign) in heaven with the saints. Let me make a few points in response to this argument (if one can call it that). In this present world we are all fractured images of God in need of a restoration that we alone cannot accomplish. This is the reason that humans can be so capable of heroic good *and* unspeakable evil. Hell represents, I suspect, an asymptotic[3] erasure of the image of the rejected Creator in the human soul.

And so, even the possibility of happiness, friendship, festivity (partying)—all of these things will be impossible because they presuppose real, if broken, goodness that is metaphysically (and probably psycholog-

---

3   A mathematical term denoting a function that is always approaching its limit but never reaching it. The idea being that the soul in hell is eternally approaching non-existence but never reaching it. This is the only way I can understand the affirmation of the Church's continual witness to the reality of hell while also acknowledging the reality that an absolute separation from God is *ipso facto* an absolute separation from being, since the ontological reality of the universe is contingent on its relationship, imperfect and fractured though it may be, with its first (and efficient and final) cause.

ically) dependent on the divine image. Let me unpack that phrase: in this age all humans, even ones who are idolaters and worship the created rather than the Creator, bear the imprint of the image and likeness of God. It is because of this—and only because of this—that they can impart and partake of good things like friendship and celebration. The souls of the damned have opted, freely, to *not be with God*, and as such, they have opted to have that divine image defaced. Indeed, they themselves have defaced it. Again, this is to say there is neither partying nor friendship in hell, because only beings that bear the image of God are capable of those things.

This strikes me as the conclusion of the Christian metanarrative: *to know God and enjoy him forever*. Here the free will of the human has been rescued and repaired in the context of the new Creation. It is unlike the childish, naive innocence of the man in Genesis 3. Here is a real, robust, and eternal righteousness wrought by God himself for us, but in a universe where death (and thus sin, a symptom of death) has been banished.

Christians have focused on the language of knowing God by employing the metaphor of *seeing* him. This is called the beatific vision and refers to a non-mediated form of knowledge. It is called "beatific" because it leads to perfect happiness and the fulfillment of the created being. In other words, the *vision* is nothing other than knowing God fully, and is thus different from knowing *about* God. The definition also clarifies that the just participate in this vision at the moment of their death, as souls in God's heaven, awaiting the resurrection of the flesh and the life everlasting. It leads to a perfect happiness because the soul is finally and completely fulfilling its *telos*—the reason for which it was created.

Many Christians (mostly Catholic and Orthodox) believe that souls of the just in God's heaven can intercede for us today, because after all there is only one Church—not two Churches: one for the dead, and one for the living. Arguing for the agency of the souls of the righteous departed we find Jesus' story about Lazarus and the rich man (Luke 16:19-31), wherein both the blessed and the damned are aware and active, or the statement in Hebrews 12:1, that "we are surrounded by such a great cloud of witnesses." Witnesses obviously must have some sort of awareness of realities on earth.

Other Christians believe that souls go into a sort of hibernation (soul sleep) as they await the resurrection of the flesh. The significance of the difference between these two alternatives should not be overstated though, as they both agree that the eternal reality of humans is as resurrected bodily beings. It is like a couple that arrives 30 minutes early for dinner reservations, and one of them wants to wait and watch the basketball game at the bar and the other wants to see if the bookstore next door has the latest issue of *Foreign Policy* or *First Things*. They both agree that the main deal is the dinner.

The Apostles' and Nicene Creeds summarize Scripture and teach that Jesus will return from heaven, judge the living and the dead (the old version says "the quick and the dead"), and his Kingdom will have no end. The act of being a king and ruling over the universe which has been purged of death is inextricably tied up with the act of governing. I suspect that humans will then be able to complete their earlier great commission (the original one, from Genesis 1:28, before death got in the way):

> God blessed them; and God said to them, "Be fruitful and multiply, and fill the earth, and subdue it; and rule over the fish of the sea and over the birds of the sky and over every living thing that moves on the earth. (Luke 16:19-31)

They have already been fruitful, and Jesus seems to preclude marriage and (one would think) procreation after the resurrection (Matthew 22:30). Through making disciples, the saints have already been fruitful and multiplied their numbers, and now they are to fill the earth and subdue it. It is not impossible that humanity would go beyond the earth and populate the whole universe. Scripture gives little information about what new mission the citizens of the Kingdom of God will have after the resurrection. But, "the dwelling place of God [will be] with man. He will dwell with them, and they will be his people, and God himself will be with them as their God" (Rev. 21:3).

Islam

If some Christians have devised amazingly complex (and entertaining) eschatologies, Islam far outshines them. Islamic eschatology (and I am leaning towards the Sunni tradition) is very clear in its concrete historicity. That is, unlike Christian eschatology, which may propose various readings of prophetic material, there is a strong consensus in Islam about what the end days leading up to the great *Yawm al Qiyama* or the Day of Resurrection (and hence judgment) will be like. My colleague and friend Brent Neely, an expert in Islamic apocalyptic literature, has compiled this list of elements associated with the end times in Islam:

> As to the portents, celestial and otherwise, yes, the "signs" are a stock-in-trade of the genre. 1. There are "sky signs" of a sort in the Qur'an (including, by some interpreters, the splitting of the moon); 2. there are portents that played a part in Islamic eschatological fervor in history; 3. then there are the portents collected in hadith, canonical and otherwise. Some of the signs relate directly to the sky, like a "pelting" or "casting" (*qadhf*) from above; eclipses; smoke; distortions in time (super long days or nights); and the great "final sign" of the sun rising in the west.
>
> There are myriad other signs of all sorts, some "greater", some "lesser", some discreet events, some general (moral dissolution, women leading men, sexual permissiveness, return of *wathaniyya* or paganism, etc.) Other signs include Dajjal (with a million signs of his own), Mahdi, Jesus, a fire in the Hijaz seen in Syria, a "swallowing" by the earth, the burning of the Ka'aba by an Ethiopian, the conquest of Jerusalem, plagues, tall buildings being built, a "Sufyani" figure, a beast called the *Dabba*, the conquest of Constantinople, and so on. Of course, many of these are tied to past events—but these are either reinterpreted or will need to recur.[4]

The main showdown in the Islamic apocalypse involves an anti-Christ figure called *al masiih al dajjaal*. This false messiah is not mentioned in the Qur'an but he is in the hadith. Indeed, we know much more about him than we know about the potential anti-Christ figure in the Bible. We know he is blind in his right eye, and his eye will bulge out like a grape;[5] he will be ruddy;[6] even Noah preached about this figure;[7] he will have the word *kafir*

---

4   Personal e-mail (Dec 2014).
5   *Sahih al Bukhari* volume 3, number 105
6   *Sahih al Bukhari* volume 9, number 242
7   *Sahih al Bukhari* volume 4, number 553

(unbeliever) written on his forehead, but only true believers will be able to see this.[8] Like the anti-Christ of the Bible he will lead many astray with his false teachings. Eventually the Dajjaal[9] will raise up a Persian army of some 70,000 soldiers.

Jesus, the Muslim prophet who was never crucified but was taken up into heaven, will descend in Damascus. He will chase down the false messiah and kill him. It is during this second advent that Jesus will vindicate the Islamic claim that he was genuinely and truly a Muslim prophet:

> Narrated Abu Huraira: Allah's Apostle said, "The Hour will not be established until the son of Mary descends amongst you as a just ruler, he will break the cross, kill the pigs, and abolish the Jizya tax. Money will be in abundance so that nobody will accept it (as charitable gifts).[10]

The abolition of the jizya implies that the People of the Book will no longer be able to live under Muslim rule, and thus must either be exiled (if indeed there is any place in the world *not* under Muslim rule), convert to Islam, or be slain. If they are exiled or slain that would explain the influx of money into the *umma's* treasury.

Jesus will then reign justly over the *umma*. According to various sources, he will take a wife, have children, go on the *hajj*, and eventually die a natural death and be buried next to the Prophet Muhammad in Medina.

I have heard Christians emphasize how much we have in common with Muslims because we all believe Jesus will return. There are indeed commonalities between Islam and Christianity but this does not strike me as one of them, precisely because one of the central reasons for Jesus' return is to refute Christianity (and Judaism) publicly and perhaps violently (implied by the abolition of the *jizya*).[11] Jesus in this eschatology functions like Allah in the Qur'an: the one who consistently vindicates the cause

---

8   *Sahih Muslim* book 41, number 7007

9   See the entry in the glossary for more details.

10   *Sahih al Bukhari* volume 3, number 656

11   Note the violence of Jesus in many Christian interpretations of his return as well. Once I asked a Muslim friend how many people Muhammad had killed. He responded, "I don't know, probably a lot!" And then I asked, "And how many has Jesus killed?" He replied, "None yet, but when he comes back who knows how many people he will kill!" I thought this was a splendid rejoinder.

of Muhammad. There are many other signs that will take place shortly
before the Day of Resurrection, as mentioned above. The return of Jesus is
not the final sign nor is it necessarily the most important of them. I outlined it here, though, because it is of special interest to Christians trying
to understand Islam.

Once these signs have taken place, the resurrection of all humanity
will take place and individuals will be judged based on the good and evil
deeds they have done. The status of Christians and Jews is difficult to discern though, for can any good deed outweigh the evil of denying the final
Prophet of Allah? Most people approaching judgment will not know their
status with God, though there are some exceptions, like those who die
waging jihad.[12] God is indeed merciful and compassionate but he is also
severe, and one has no way of knowing with confidence what the disposi-
tion of Allah will be at the judgment.

However, there is an interesting hadith about salvation:

> Abu Huraira reported Allah's Messenger (may peace be upon him) as
> saying: I shall be pre-eminent amongst the descendants of Adam on
> the Day of Resurrection and I will be the first intercessor and the first
> whose intercession will be accepted (by Allah).[13]

The implication is that Muhammad will intercede before God for his own
people. This is not the same thing as vicarious atonement, where Jesus *dies*
for people's sins, thus *atoning* for them, but there is a clear impression that
if a person is on the borderline between the garden (*janna*) and the fire,
then this intercession is very important.

But consider also this fascinating hadith:

> Narrated 'Um al-'Ala: An Ansari woman who gave the pledge of alle-
> giance to the Prophet that the Ansar drew lots concerning the dwelling
> of the Emigrants. 'Uthman bin Maz'un was decided to dwell with them
> (i.e. Um al-'Ala's family), 'Uthman fell ill and I nursed him till he died,
> and we covered him with his clothes.

---

12   *Sahih al Bukhari* Book 93, Number 555
13   *Sahih Muslim* Book 30, Number 5655

Then the Prophet came to us and I (addressing the dead body) said, "O Abu As-Sa'ib, may Allah's Mercy be on you! I bear witness that Allah has honored you." On that the Prophet said, "How do you know that Allah has honored him?" I replied, "I do not know. May my father and my mother be sacrificed for you, O Allah's Apostle! But who else is worthy of it (if not 'Uthman)?"

He said, "As to him, by Allah, death has overtaken him, and I hope the best for him. **By Allah, though I am the Apostle of Allah, yet I do not know what Allah will do to me.**" By Allah, I will never assert the piety of anyone after him. That made me sad, and when I slept I saw in a dream a flowing stream for 'Uthman bin Maz'un. I went to Allah's Apostle and told him of it. He remarked, "That symbolizes his (good) deeds."[14]

Here is a man who is clearly unsure of his own eternal fate.

All in all, then, the question of final judgment and the value of the intercession of Muhammad (or other prophets or holy men) cannot be answered decisively. I do not think Christians should gloat over this, because our own Scriptures are sometimes very precise and demanding in terms of what is required to be saved at the final judgment. Romans 10:9 seems to demand an unequivocal verbal pronunciation, Mark 16:16 appears to add a water baptism to the requisites for salvation, 1 John 1:19 appears to require a regular confession of sins in addition to the original confession of faith, and 1 John 2:4 appears to set an extraordinarily high bar of righteousness for the believer. On the other hand, there are minimalist, essentialist readings, like the thief on the cross or the very inclusive verse from Joel which is quoted often in the New Testament: "Whosoever calls on the name of the Lord shall be saved" (2:32). There have been many attempts of determining what is the minimum one must do to be saved, but even asking a question about "What is the least one can do to be saved" is itself a question that Jesus or the Apostles would never have countenanced. For them the question was always, what *else* can you do to live out your salvation?

Similarly, among Muslims, I have met some that are very anxious about the Day of Judgment because they have missed daily prayers a few

---

14   *Sahih al Bukhari* Vol 5, Number 266

times. But I have met others who openly invited me to Islam advertising that "the religion is easy, for every good deed during Ramadan is worth more than a bad deed done during the rest of the year; so if you keep the fast and are good for one month a year, then you can be pretty confident that your good deeds will outweigh your bad ones." There is also a strong tradition that keeping the Ramadan fast or making *hajj* will lead to a complete absolution of all sins committed up to that point of one's life. Nonetheless, it is impossible to know with certainty one's own fate, no matter how devout one has been.[15]

We learn a great deal about the destinies of the just and the damned from the Qur'an and the hadith. We know the just and the damned will dwell in intentionally created places that already exist. In former ages it was even thought that one might be able to find the entrance to Gehenna (Hell) somewhere in Yemen.[16]

As to eternal felicity, it is represented as a garden or *janna* and is sometimes also called *paradise*, an ancient Persian word that means "a walled enclosure" (with a garden in it):

> A similitude of the Garden which is promised unto those who keep their duty (to Allah): Underneath it rivers flow; its food is everlasting, and its shade; this is the reward of those who keep their duty, while the reward of disbelievers is the Fire. (13:35, Pickthall)

Furthermore, there is no rancor or toiling there, the pious will be greeted by angels, and they will never be expelled from there. There is cool drink; plenteous fruit; the men have modest, virginal female companions with them (55:56); and they will recline on "couches lined with silk brocade" (55:54). The Qur'an is explicit that the gardens of the pious are precisely those of Eden (38:50). And this brings us back to our quest to understand the Islamic metanarrative: after their original mistake, God made Adam and his wife leave the Garden of Eden. The whole of history has been a

---

15 This is not our main topic here, but it is interesting to note that one reason that some people convert from Islam to Christianity is precisely because there is a sense of security, that "we approach God's throne of grace with great confidence" (Hebrews 4:16).

16 This is to differentiate the eschatological Gehenna from the Valley of [the Sons of] Hinnom, an actual valley outside of Jerusalem's Old City.

testing ground to see who will be allowed to return to those gardens: "And Allah hath created the heavens and the earth with truth, and that every soul may be repaid what it hath earned. And they will not be wronged" (45:22, Sahih International).

There is also an interesting hadith about Allah's preparation of paradise and Gehenna. This hadith, because it reports the speech of God outside of the Qur'an, belongs to a special category of hadith called *qudsi*:

> The Messenger of Allah (peace be upon him) said: "When Allah created Paradise and Hell-fire, He sent Gabriel to Paradise, saying: Look at it and at what I have prepared therein for its inhabitants. The Prophet (peace be upon him) said: So he came to it and looked at it and at what Allah had prepared therein for its inhabitants. [. . .] So [Gabriel] returned to Him and said: By your glory, no one hears of it without entering it. So He ordered that it be encompassed by forms of hardship [ie, rigorous devotions], and He said: Return to it and look at what I have prepared therein for its inhabitants. [. . .] So [Gabriel] returned to it and found that it was encompassed by forms of hardship. Then he returned to Him and said: By Your glory, I fear that no one will enter it. He said: Go to Hell-fire and look at it and what I have prepared therein for its inhabitants, and he found that it was in layers, one above the other. Then he returned to Him and said: By Your glory, no one who hears of it will enter it. So He ordered that it be encompassed by lusts. Then He said: Return to it. And he returned to it and said: By Your glory, I am frightened that no one will escape from entering it."[17]

This account reiterates in greater detail the tenet that human history is a testing ground. Unlike in the Christian metanarrative, Allah and his angels are actively involved in the preparation and maintenance of paradise and Gehenna. In the Christian metanarrative, Hell is an unnatural state of being—something that does not have a positive existence of its own. CS Lewis, in his masterful *The Great Divorce*, likened this to a crack in the ground.

---

17   Hadith Qudsi 38, on the authority of Abu Huraira, present in Abu Daoud's collection.

In Islam, sex is one of the main gifts that God bestows unto the pious men. As to women, it is not clear what their role or reward is in paradise. There is a strong tradition in Christianity that judges this as a carnal vision of eternal felicity—endless sex, rivers of wine, comfort and prosperity, friendship and festivity. Maybe it is carnal—but what is so bad about that? The Islamic vision of the eschaton certainly connects with the masculine soul in a way that the Church's formulation of its own eschatology does not. In other words, I suspect that in many cases a sensual eternity is an asset of Islam, and not a liability—at least when it comes to men.

We also learn about Gehenna or, as it is sometimes simply called, The Fire (al nar). It's fire is much hotter than earthly fire, the food of its residents is the tree of Zaqqum, and it contains more women than men.[18] Not only will sinners reside in the Fire, but also disbelieving jinn (genies). Allah has appointed specific angels to be wardens of the souls in Gehenna,[19] and the residents of Gehenna have been cursed by Allah, the angels, and all of humanity.[20] The fuel of Hell is men and stones.[21] We also hear of some punishments used in Gehenna: "Those who reject Our Signs, We shall soon cast into the Fire. As often as their skins are roasted through, We shall change them for fresh skins, that they may taste the penalty. For Allah is Exalted in Power, Wise" (4:55-56). In a dream, one of Muhammad's companions saw that it was like a deep well, with men suspended upside down, and guarded by angels with iron maces.[22] In another passage we read of scalding water being poured on the heads of the residents of Gehenna.[23]

The eschatological vision of Islam reveals the justice and magnanimity of God, who rules over both the Garden (al janna) and the Fire. His kindness and pleasure is shown by the happiness and plenitude of life experienced by the few who enter the Garden but also by the wailing and torment of those who did not worship him alone and obey his Prophet. After

---

18   *Sahiih al Bukhari* Number 3241, *Sahiih Muslim* Number 2737. Before the Christian gloats, he should address the last verses of Ecclesiastes 7 wherein the author states that he found only one man among a thousand who were wise, but not a single woman among those thousand.

19   74:31

20   2:161, 162

21   2:24

22   *Sahiih Al Bukhari* Vol 9, Number 155

23   22:19-22

the final judgment balance will have been restored to the universe and those living in the Garden live according to his eternal will, the shari'a. In this sense the final result is indeed a profound and universal peace. Those who would not live according to this divine will—the shari'a—experience eternal punishment meted out by his angels in the place of Fire. A dramatic eschatological separation of the obedient from the disobedient at the Day of Resurrection has sufficed to restore the original balance. Every human, regardless of whether blessed or damned, thus fulfills its *telos*: to know Allah's power, and in so doing to worship him: "And I have not created the Jinn and man but that they worship Me" (51:57).

But what of the devil? The one who at first opposed Allah and would not bow down before Adam? Recall that after this confrontation the devil told God, "Seest Thou this (creature) whom Thou hast honoured above me, if Thou give me grace until the Day of Resurrection I verily will seize his seed, save but a few" (17:62). Here is a contest! That until the Day of Resurrection the devil would tempt and snatch as many of these supposedly lofty creatures as he could—a creature so lofty that Allah had commanded even the devil to bow down before him.

But then consider the response of Allah to this challenge:

> Go, and whosoever of them followeth thee - lo! hell will be your payment, ample payment. And excite any of them whom thou canst with thy voice, and urge thy horse and foot against them, and be a partner in their wealth and children, and promise them. Satan promiseth them only to deceive. Lo! My (faithful) bondmen - over them thou hast no power, and thy Lord sufficeth as (their) guardian. (17:63-65, Pickthall)

Allah accepts the challenge, though after the Day of Resurrection the devil, and all who follow him, will find their abode in Gehenna. It does not come across in the English, but the Arabic is clear that "your payment" is in the plural—you (the devil) and all who follow you. Nonetheless, the devil is given free rein to tempt and lure the humans. However, over Allah's bondsmen—the Arabic is 'abiid which usually is best translated as *slaves*—the devil has no power.

In the eschaton the challenge is concluded. The devil has indeed led a greater part of humanity to the Fire, but even in this Allah is glorified.

Furthermore, the devil himself is, presumably, now in the Fire, unable to tempt the slaves of Allah who worship and enjoy his favor in the Garden. This is perhaps the secret reason that Allah had in creating man—that they would be able to enjoy Allah's munificence in a bodily and material manner unavailable to the angels:

> And when thy Lord said unto the angels: Lo! I am about to place a viceroy in the earth, they said: Wilt thou place therein one who will do harm therein and will shed blood, while we, we hymn Thy praise and sanctify Thee? He said: Surely I know that which ye know not. (2:30, Pickthall)

Allah already had angels to worship him, so why create humans as well? What could the humans do that the angels could not? Or, how could Allah be glorified by humans in a way that the angels could not glorify him? Humans, in their very carnal and sensual physicality, have an avenue of worship of the divine being that the angels and the jinn, being essentially incorporeal, do not. In the Christian metanarrative, humans were made in the image and likeness of God and given free will, and so they could love him *if they chose to.*

The two visions of the eschaton, then, are inextricably tied to the teleological anthropologies in their very different Creation narratives. Both visions of the eschaton propose a bodily resurrection and a full knowledge of God, with Christianity focusing on God's love and Islam focusing on his power. For this to happen, Christianity requires the incarnation, the Cross, the Resurrection, and finally a new Creation. In Islam the problem was much lighter—there was the challenge of the devil, which Allah accepted; the devil tempted and lured people, making them ignorant of God's will. God responded with messengers and prophets, culminating in Muhammad, his Qur'an and his *umma*—a community that is irreducibly both political and "religious," simultaneously an imperial religion and a religious empire.

The mission of the Church that Jesus founded is to offer Jesus' message of divine reconciliation—the Gospel—to all the peoples of the earth in preparation for the eschaton. The mission of the *umma* is to get an upper hand on the devil's schemes by enjoining the right and prohibiting the evil, acquiring the civil power to do so when possible—through migration, fertility, *da'wa*, or jihad. In doing this, the *umma* would prepare the world for the eschaton. The Church is unlike the *umma* because while it has a code of ethical conduct, it has no shari'a. The Church has no one, detailed biblical prescription as to how it should relate to the civil authority beyond that the Church must never be *identical* to the civil authority, lest its mission be compromised.[24] Conversely, the mission of the *umma* is ultimately accomplished through the absorption of all civil power into the divinely revealed and immutable shari'a governing the entirety of human society. The Church then may invite, but not compel; the *umma* by divine and just necessity may and, at times, must compel.

Discussion Questions

What is the Muslim vision of Jesus' role in the eschaton?

The author mentions several times that Islam connects to the masculine soul s as a positive aspect of Islam that Christianity lacks somewhat. If Islam connects with the masculine soul, shouldn't it also connect with the feminine soul? And if not, why not? And if it doesn't, is it really an asset, as the author alleges?

---

24   This is not to say that some Christians have not envisioned a close and harmonious cooperation between the church and the state, which is a political ideology that has an august and illustrious past, especially in the Byzantine Empire. But even then, and even at the height of papal power in the West, there was no effort to completely and seamlessly merge the two into one.

Nine

CONCLUSION

I started by arguing for abandoning the category of religion as a basis for comparing Islam and Christianity and instead opting for a comparative study of their metanarratives. After observing that their protologies appear similar I argued that they propose different anthropologies, with humans being created for differing reasons. In Islam it is to know the power of God, and in Christianity to know his love. Both agree that the worship of the Creator is essential to the human *telos*. The fundamental bifurcation in the two metanarratives, though, emerges at the point of hamartiology: Christianity claiming that the entry of death through sin into the universe is the fundamental problem in the metanarrative, with Islam presenting the divine contest between God and the devil, who himself will utilize the strategy of *ignorance* or *jahiliyya* to debar people from knowing God's commands and obeying them. In the Christian metanarrative the rebellion of man is of such depth that humanity's alienation from God becomes communal and communicative: original sin. In Islam the rebellion results in expulsion from the Garden, though the original innocence of humans is retained. Those who obey God's commands will, in the end, return to the Garden.

In the Christian metanarrative Israel is called by God to live faithfully according to the Torah. This faithfulness to the Torah would attract the attention of the peoples and tribes around Israel who would learn God's will through Israel. Israel, however, was not faithful to this covenant. While the Qur'an has much less information about Israel than the Bible, the Islamic metanarrative likewise castigates Israel for a lack of faithfulness to their covenant with God, and this in spite of the fact that the Sons of Israel received so many more messengers and prophets than did other people of the earth.

The Christian metanarrative is not ready to give up on Israel, though, and Jesus of Nazareth is faithful to the covenant and so reconstitutes Israel. He announces the Kingdom of God, inviting people to repent, and through his blood shed on the cross ratifies a new covenant that secures the forgiveness of sins for his disciples. Before the summation of human history (the eschaton), it is necessary that every tribe and tongue and nation be afforded the opportunity to enter into his Kingdom through repentance. With this objective in mind he initiates a movement and founds a community that is given the generic name *ekklesia*, meaning *assembly* or *gathering*. This community is given a code of conduct, rite of initiation, rite of memorial, mission statement, leadership, growth strategy (discipleship), and God's very Spirit to animate and empower it.

The metanarrative of Islam acknowledges that Jesus was a prophet, but insists that Christians misunderstood and distorted his message and ministry. In the metanarrative of Islam the problem is not death and there is no original sin, so an atoning death on a cross is superfluous and bizarre. Furthermore, the divine texts revealed to Moses, David, and Jesus had been corrupted and could not be relied upon to instruct people to live according to God's eternal and wise will for human society—the shari'a.

What was needed, according to the Islamic metanarrative, was a seal of the prophets—someone who would bring the clear and incorruptible divine law to humanity, and Muhammad carried out this role. In every word and deed of this man God revealed his will for humanity, and God sent him a divine book free of errors and corruptions (like the previous books). God's will for humanity was, like the Torah, comprehensive, including instructions on topics as broad as banking, eating, marriage, war and peace, diplomacy, medicine, the end of human history, dress, criminal law, will and testaments, and much more. The community animated by Muhammad was called the *umma* and it was given the mission to enjoin the right and forbid the wrong, and to do this until the end of world. The methods for carrying out its mission were broader than those given to the Church, for, in addition to preaching, the *umma* could, and perhaps must, use the power of the sword if needed to enjoin the right and forbid the wrong.

The Church of Jesus may work with the civil authority, or it may, at times, need to work in spite of it. However, the Kingdom heralded by Jesus can never be identical to any of the kingdoms of this world—so deeply infected by death through sin is the cosmos. The Islamic metanarrative is much more optimistic, for its problem is much lighter, and in it humans remain basically good. And so, the Islamic metanarrative both envisions and prescribes that the *umma* can and should instate the Kingdom and law of God here and now.

The communities today are carrying out their missions with varying degrees of success. Both faiths are growing numerically, but numerical growth alone should not be confused with success in relation to their respective missions. I also argued at some length that the future of Western Europe will be strongly influenced, and maybe dominated, by the Islamic metanarrative in many of its urban centers. I provided evidence based on demographics and migration patterns to support this hypothesis. The demise of the West is not to be interpreted as the end of Christianity, though.

Both metanarratives propose a final judgment. In Islam the blessed return to the original felicity of the Garden, with the damned being tortured by God's angels in hell. In Christianity hell is a paradoxical reality—but one necessitated by God's respect for free will. All humanity will spend eternity with its god: and that may be the soul's Creator or the soul's self. There is a consensus among Muslims and Christians that the devil will be cast into the eternal fire of hell. The Church, having fulfilled its mission to the peoples of the world, will then gather together in praise of God, with people from every tribe, tongue, and nation. The state of the blessed is summed up as seeing God and knowing him, restating the relational aspect of Christian anthropology. In the eschaton the newness of Jesus' resurrected body will spread throughout the whole universe resulting in its *apocatastasis*—its rebirth or renewal or "the restoration of all things" (Acts 3:21).

I want to be transparent about my own position on all of this. I am, obviously, a Christian. I am not afraid of Islam or Muslims. I believe that the Church of Jesus will continue to the end of the age because he promised it.

I hope that I am as critical of Christianity as I am of Islam, and I see the *umma* doing a number of things correctly that I don't see the Church, by and large, doing correctly. I also believe that Islam has a future, whereas Western Civilization is in an irreversible state of decline. I am not too sad about this because the West, I believe, has ceased to fulfill the *telos* of a civilization.[1]

Second: there are a couple of topics I intentionally chose not to address, primarily free will and the sovereignty of God. Plenty of Christians and Muslims would disagree with me, but I feel pretty confident in saying that both the Bible and the Qur'an insist that humans have a genuine free will while God is also sovereign over all of history. That is an apparent paradox I am comfortable with, but many Muslims and Christians are not and feel compelled to tip the scale to one side or the other: human or divine agency. I do not. I will simply agree with Luther on this: "If you're going to heaven, thank God; if you're going to Hell, thank yourself."

Third: everyone needs to make a decision. Christianity and Islam are the future, and if people want to belong to a community that is not un-naturally deselecting itself from existence (secular humanism, atheism), these are the strong horses. I heard an undergrad student complaining that she prays and believes in God but doesn't go to church because it is "full of hypocrites." Here is how I respond to that student (and I do this sooner or later every semester, in every class): What is hypocritical is for a person to profit from Christians—by receiving an education in a Christian school, being nourished in a city founded by Christian missionaries, like San Antonio, being born or cared for in a hospital founded by Christians, or being fed and clothed by Christian charities—and yet you will not go to be with those Christians to worship your Creator? And this is because some of them are hypocrites? Of course Christians fail to live up to their moral aspirations. But the person issuing the complaint is the true hypocrite. I bring this up because I have challenged the reader to seriously consider either Christianity or Islam as a committed way of life. Since the

---

1   It is true that this also means to a significant degree the demise of liberal democracy, with rule of law, private property, protection of rights, and religious freedom. Because they lead to human flourishing, as history has proved, should I not be sad about that? My hope is that eventually, among the breakage, something new and fresh and more authentic and contoured more closely to the real core of the human experience will one day emerge—but that is far from guaranteed.

charge of hypocrisy against the Church is so common, I felt a rebuttal was necessary.

Fourth: Jihad and the Crusades. This is yet another common fallacy: *all religions have violence, Islam has the jihads today like Christians had the Crusades.* Here is the historical truth about the Crusades. They were Christian attempts to imitate what Muslims had been so successful at— holy war or sacralized violence. It took a few centuries, but the Church realized that it just could not integrate (syncretize is the precise word) sacred, martial violence into its common life. Here is Bernard Lewis of Princeton on the Crusades and Jihad:

> The *jihad* was a sacred mission enjoined by scripture and incorporated into the holy law, to continue until all the world was open to the light of Islam. The crusade was a human enterprise, not enjoined—some might rather say forbidden—by Christian scripture, and undertaken for a limited purpose, to defend, or, where lost, to recover Christian territories.[2]

Fifth: the argument that jihad and Islamic 'terrorism' can be traced back to the Crusades is flawed. Here is Thomas Madden, one of the world's foremost scholars of the Crusades, commenting on this argument:

> The truth is that medieval Muslims came to realize the Crusades were religious but had little interest in them. When, in 1291, Muslim armies removed the last vestiges of the Crusader Kingdom from Palestine, the Crusades largely dropped out of Muslim memory.[3]

Sixth: how you should react to the Islamic future of Europe and Canada. I'm not afraid of Islam. I lived in Muslim-majority cities for years and generally felt content and safe. A Christian response to Islam cannot be based on fear, "for God gave us a spirit not of fear but of power and love and self-control" (2 Timothy 1:7). The Christian response to the growth of Islam in Europe (in all its non-monolithic and scintillating variety) must

---

2   'Europe and Islam' in *From Babel to Dragomans*, 2004.
3   'Inventing the Crusades' in *First Things* (Summer 2009), p 43.

be one of love. For love is the secret weapon of the Christian faith. And no, I don't mind talking about Christians having weapons. It is a weapon of the weak, and thus a powerful one. This is the point of Tolkien (a devout Catholic) recruiting a weak hobbit to destroy the Ring of Power. The God of the Christian metanarrative is like that—utilizing weak things to glorify himself and communicate his love, putting the treasure of his Spirit into humble jars of clay.

Seventh: my personal feeling about why Islam is unworkable is that it misunderstands man. The basic tenet that humans are born good and that the problem is ignorance of God's will (or just lack of education in general)[4] is untenable. Each and every human has had the experience of having chosen what was wrong even though he knew unreservedly and completely that what he was doing would hurt him and the people he loved. I don't see Islam (or secular humanism, modernity, or atheism) as having any way of explaining this that does not end up being self-referentially incoherent.[5] Consider: the shari'a has been defined in detail now for many centuries, and today there are dozens of countries that are governed by some form of the shari'a. Yet not a single one of these can be pointed to as an example of the just and prosperous society that Islam promises.

The great insight of the Christian metanarrative is summed up in the frumpy word "concupiscence," meaning that human will is somehow broken and turned inwards on itself. It means that the human will has a tendency towards the wrong that cannot simply be explained away by ignorance—for this desire is often opposed to, and victorious over, reason. This reality has been summed up by Jesus, who said, "The spirit indeed is willing, but the flesh is weak" (Mk 14:38), and by Paul, who wrote, "For I do not understand my own actions. For I do not do what I want, but I do the very thing I hate." (Rom 7:15). The Christian metanarrative, therefore, has the capacity to account for the reality that humans are capable of both great good and great evil.

Eighth: I dismiss liberal Christianity too lightly. How can I simply say that liberal or progressive theology "does not matter"? I can say it because right now I belong to one of the most liberal, progressive denominations

---

4   As the metanarrative of atheistic secular humanism proposes. That metanarrative and the one of Islam are very close to each other once the surface is penetrated, I think.

5   That is, it sets out a standard of truth that it cannot meet.

in the world, The Episcopal Church (USA), and I have seen it from the inside. Many of our people and clergy are fine Christians, and there is hope for them, but the structure as a whole, if it does not change, has no future. There is ample evidence to support what I have alleged—that liberal Christianity is in a state of irreversible numerical decline.

T. S. Eliot wrote, "In my end is my beginning." I do hope that arriving at the end of this book represents a beginning of further reflection and action. I hope that this book has helped the Christian reader to understand how powerful, attractive, and compelling the metanarrative of Islam can be. For the non-religious reader, I hope you will consider the two options and embrace God thoughtfully through whichever one you find more convincing. It is obvious that I find the Christian metanarrative to be more fulfilling, consistent, and beautiful, not just because it tells the truth about God, but because it allows for us to make sense of ourselves—our great capacity for good living side by side with our great capacity for evil. In the case that a Muslim has read this book, I extend to you an invitation to be reconciled to your Creator, but according to the path that Jesus son of Mary presented to us, and to acknowledge that commitment by public baptism at a local congregation of his disciples.

Discussion Questions

The author has opined that Islam and Christianity are similar in both acknowledging the reality of free will and the sovereignty of God. Some readers have disagreed, saying that Islam leans away from a genuine free will and that Christianity tends towards preserving and respecting each human's free will. What do you think?

How can a Christian response to Islam not be based on fear in view of the belief and practice of the "Medina Muslims"?

Given the material in this chapter, what is your response to the Islam of the Islamic State (aka, ISIS)?

The author has been intentional about not proposing political responses to Islam. But given what you have learned, what would you propose?

GLOSSARY

Abrahamic Faiths: Judaism, Christianity and Islam. An attempt to establish a foundational commonality between the three faiths by claiming that all three find their roots in the person of Abraham; a Western psychological and rhetorical strategy.

Abrogation: a principle of Islamic hermeneutics whereby historically later verses from the Qur'an cancel/abrogate earlier verses.

Allah: the Arabic word for God. Etymologically related to the Hebrew words *El* and *Elohim* from the Old Testament.

Atheism: the conviction that the evidence against the existence of God is more convincing than the evidence in favor of God's existence.

Bible: in Christianity, the collection of created, human writings uniquely inspired by God's Spirit; the written Word of God that testifies to the incarnate Word of God. For Islam's version see *corruption.*

Bifurcate: verb, the branching of one thing into two or more things of the same nature, as in a path that bifurcates.

Caliph: the successor of the Prophet and head of the *umma.*

Caliphate: the office of the caliph. The last widely-accepted caliphate was abolished in 1924. Large portions of the shari'a cannot be carried out when it is vacant.

Chthonic: of Greek origin, earthy, subterranean, associated with the underworld.

Church: the community of the New Covenant; the outward and visible gathering of men that unveils the hidden and invisible Kingdom of God. May refer to the community extending throughout history and the world, or may be used to refer to a particular gathering of Jesus' disciples identified by their practice and teaching of his ethics, sacraments, and doctrine. Founded by Jesus in order to announce the Gospel to all the peoples of the earth.

Circumambulate: to walk around something, as Muslims do with the Ka'ba in Mecca during their pilgrimage or *hajj.*

Concupiscence: Christianity: noun, an innate and irrational tendency towards the misuse of free will; a result of the rebellion of our first ancestors.

Conflate: verb, fusing items into one entity.

Corruption: Arabic, *tahriif.* The doctrine common to most Muslims that the texts of the Torah, Psalms and Gospel have been irretrievably corrupted by Jews and Christians.

Da'wa: Islam: to call, or calling, as in calling or inviting a person to receive Islam, or to practice Islam more devoutly. Similar to the Christian term *evangelism.*

Dajjaal: Islam: a false messiah who will deceive many of the faithful. We have extensive details on his appearance and he will have the word *kafir* (unbeliever) written on his forehead. He will be defeated in an apocalyptic battle.

Death: Christianity: the fundamental problem of the metanarrative; a dysteliological or entropic principal suffusing the Creation, compromising but not obliterating its ontological traces of its first and efficient cause.

Dhimmi: Islam: a community of theists under Islamic rule. They have a treaty of protection with the Muslim ruler that may be revoked without notification by the Muslim ruler. Such peoples are required to pay the *jizya*.

Discipleship: teaching by modeling; Jesus' prescribed method for ensuring that the Gospel will reach all the peoples of the earth in preparation for his *paraousia* and the *eschaton*.

Election: Christianity: a quality of the Trinitarian bond between the Father and the Son; the Son is the elect of the Father and those joined to the Son share in this election. The refraction of this ontological election in Scripture is witnessed in instances of God's choice of a person or community to fulfill a certain role for the sake of others.

Eschaton: a Greek word meaning *end*. In Islam and Christianity it is the summation of human history and is characterized by the judgment of all humanity—the living and the dead.

Etymology: a chronological account of the birth and development of a particular word or element of a word

Fecund: adjective, the quality, especially of females, of producing offspring in substantial numbers.

Final Cause: see *Telos*.

Gospel: Christianity: the good news that one can prepare for the coming of God's kingdom by repenting and being baptized. In doing this one not only is spared the judgment of this Kingdom, but becomes a citizen and agent of it. Repentance secures forgiveness due to the efficacy of the New Covenant. To assure that this message would be announced to all the peoples of the earth, Jesus initiated a movement called the *Church*. See also *Kingdom of God* and *injiil*.

Hadith: The plural in English may be either hadith or hadiths: An Arabic word referring to a saying or an event from the life of Muhammad or one of his companions. While various collections of hadith exist, collections by certain scholars (Al Bukhari, Abu Daoud, Muslim, etc.) are considered authentic (Arabic: *sahiih*) and form the foundation of the shari'a. References to specific hadith are made by referring to the name of the collator with a reference number (as opposed to a page number).

Hallal: Arabic, adjective, meaning *permitted* or *lawful*. It is a category of the shari'a denoting what Allah allows Muslims to do. For instance: eating the flesh of all things from the sea is *hallal*, taking a Jewish or Christian wife is *hallal*, sex with slave women is *hallal*. See also *haram*.

Hamartiology: The study of sin.

Haram: Arabic, adjective, meaning *forbidden* or *unlawful*. It is a category of the shari'a denoting what Allah forbids. For instance: eating pork is *haram*, the marriage of a Muslim woman to a Christian or Jewish man is *haram*, apostasy from Islam is *haram*. There is a further category of deeds which are discouraged, but are not forbidden. See also *hallal*.

Hedonism: an ordering of life or ethic wherein pleasure (not truth, not virtue, not race, not nation, not God) is considered to be the greatest good and pain/discomfort is the bad to be avoided. Late modern humans tend to, without really thinking about it, default to some sort of hedonistic construction of values and meaning.

Humanism: any metanarrative that is mistakenly and naively optimistic about the moral goodness of man and his capacity to instate of justly ordered society through reason.

Iblis: the proper name of the devil in the Qur'an (as opposed to Satan in the Christian tradition). Possibly derived from the Greek word *diabolos*. There is no consensus in Islamic thought whether Iblis is a jinn or a rebellious angel.

Ignorance: See *jahiliyya*

Increate: adjective, never having been created.

Injiil: Arabic, ultimately derived from the Greek word *evangelion*, meaning "good news". In Islam, the name of the book given by Allah to Prophet Jesus, in which he foretells the coming of Muhammad. The *injiil* given to Jesus by Allah is lost to us today. See also *corruption* and *Gospel*.

Irenic: adjective, antonym of polemic, characterized by good will and authentic communication. Preferred over the word *peaceful* in this book because *peaceful* is often misunderstood as meaning characterized by a lack of violence.

Islam: Arabic for *submission*.

Israel: the one who struggles with man and God, for man and God.

Jahiliyya: an Arabic word meaning *ignorance*. Islam: It is the fundamental problem in the metanarrative of Islam, whereby people, who are born good and in proper relation to the Creator, go astray. It is a tool of the devil/*iblis* who has pledged to lead people astray until the Day of Judgment. The problem is remedied by God's revelation of his shari'a in the Qur'an and the life of the Prophet. See *shari'a*.

Janna: Arabic for *garden*. In Islam, the setting of original felicity and the reward for the believers after the resurrection. Also called *paradise*.

Jesus: Christianity: A prophet from the Galilean village of Nazareth whose mission was the reconstitution of Israel and the proclamation that the Kingdom of God was drawing near. The person in whom the divine nature of the Son was hypostatically united to a human nature derived from his mother. In Islam: A Muslim prophet who was sent exclusively to the Jewish people, born of a virgin, performed miracles, did not die but was taken into heaven, and will return prior to the eschaton to vindicate Muhammad and Islam.

Jihad: Islam, a struggle for God. In the Qur'an it refers to fighting against enemies of God, and since God and Muhammad in Islam are functionally coterminous, any enemy of Muhammad or his *umma*, must be the object of jihad. There is a wide variety of opinions among Muslims today regarding who precisely constitutes an "enemy" and thus a legitimate target of the *umma's* jihad/struggle. The ultimate purpose of jihad is that all the world submit to God and his shari'a.

Jinn: in Islam, creatures made of fire, capable of both good and evil, who have received the preaching of prophets, and are capable of repenting.

According to Islamic tradition King Solomon the prophet was capable of speaking with this creatures. Related to the English word *genie*.

Jizya: an important source of income for the *umma* at some times. A tax paid by the people of the book in order for them to secure the precarious status of *dhimmi*. Allowed for them sometimes to survive under Islamic rule, but with inferior rights to Muslims, even if they were a majority of the population.

Kingdom of God: Christianity: the invisible reconstituting energy of God active in the cosmos, fully present now but unseen as the god of this world has blinded humanity to its reality. Men may prepare for its full unveiling at the *paraousia* by repenting and being baptized. For some its unveiling will be one of judgment and damnation, for others it will be of life and joy. Repentance secures forgiveness of sins because of the efficacy of the New Covenant. The Church is the outward and visible sign of the invisible Kingdom of God.

Late Modernity: a paradoxical metanarrative that claims there is no such thing as a metanarrative.

Metanarrative: a story that subsumes and explains and interprets all other stories.

Missiology: Christianity: this is a mongrel word, combining unnaturally a Latin root with a Greek one, and thus likely of American origin. Meaning the study of the methods, practice, theology and history of the Church as it is has participated in the mission of God.

Muhammad: Islam: the seal of the prophets and the ideal man, whose every action was a revelation of God's shari'a, and who was used by God to reveal his final and incorruptible

message of the Qur'an. Christianity: at best, a prophetic visionary who called Arabs away from polytheistic paganism to monotheism; at worst, a power hungry man who received verses from the devil (in the guise of Gabriel) and who led countless people away from God's love revealed in Jesus Christ.

New Covenant: the evolution and summation of God's covenants with Abraham, Israel and David. Ratified by the shedding of blood at Christ's crucifixion, Christ being the mediator of this covenant. The covenant that God made with the Apostles and "many", securing for them the forgiveness of sins and the inscription of God's law on their hearts through the indwelling of the Holy Spirit, which is God's response to the problem of concupiscence. The community of the New Covenant is the Church; in the sacrament of Communion the Church remembers Christ's suffering and announces his future *parousia*.

PBUH: "Peace be upon him"; a traditional invocation used by Muslims after the name of a prophet is mentioned. The invocation used after Muhammad's name is mentioned is different, and can roughly be translated, "May the prayer and peace of God be upon him."

Parousia: Greek for *presence, arrival* or *official visit.* Christianity: the bodily return of Jesus Christ to earth to judge the living and the dead and unveil completely the reality of his indestructible and eternal Kingdom. See also *Kingdom of God* and *eschaton.*

Polity: derived from the Greek word for city, *polis,* it refers to the instantiation of a constellation of symbols and practices whereby a community or group of communities is governed.

Post-modernity: see *Late Modernity.*

Protology: the science of beginnings.

Qur'an: an Arabic word of uncertain derivation, though many suppose it means *recitation*. In Islam: the increate and eternal word of God communicated to Muhammad through the mediation of an angel. Along with the life of Muhammad it is the foundation for the shari'a.

Religion: the form of justice wherein man engages in the impossible task of rendering unto God his due.

Sacrament: an outward and visible sign of an inward and invisible grace; or, a sign that accomplishes and effectuates what it points to.

Sahiih (Sahih): an Arabic characterization of certain hadith that are considered to be authentic. See also *hadith*.

Secular Humanism: a coercive metanarrative characterized by a misconstrual of the nature of freedom wherein each individual human constructs, deconstructs, or refuses to construct his own individual and, ultimately, subjective set of meanings and values and poltity.

Science: a coherent and ordered body of knowledge about a particular topic (God, humanity, living beings).

Shari'a: God's eternal and immutable will governing all human affairs (political, ethical, fiduciary, dietary, sartorial, etc.), encapsulated in the Qur'an and Muhammad's day to day life, and codified by practitioners of *usul al fiqh* (the derivation of Islamic jurisprudence).

Shirk: Arabic for *association*; Islam: a grave sin whereby a created thing is associated with the increate deity.

Sura or Surah: a chapter of the Qur'an. Citations to the Qur'an may name the surah (Al Baqara, or in English, *The Cattle)* and then the verse, or may list the number of the surah (2 to refer to the Qur'an second Surah) and then the verse.

Tawhiid: Islamic monotheism, wherein God's self-experience is solitary, ultimately simple, monadic and non-communal. As opposed to Trinitarian monotheism wherein God's self-experience is in a plurality of experiential and active modes. The most important difference between the two theories of monotheism is that the monadic deity of *tawhiid* cannot be essentially loving, for love is the virtue whereby the good of the other is placed above the good of one's self.

Telos: Philosophy: the reason for which a thing exists, its final cause, the answer to the question, *what is it for* or *why does it exist?*

Terrorism: inducing fear in a population by the strategic deployment of coercive power of the threat thereof to effectuate political and/or spiritual change.

TFR (Total Fertility Rate): the average number of children that would be born to a woman of a given population if she were to survive from birth to the end of her reproductive life.

Trinity: Christianity: the revelation of God's eternal experience of his own being in reference to this Creation. Islam: at best a confusing and nonsensical doctrine; at worse the sin of *shirk*. Compare to *tawhiid* above.

Umma: Islam: the unity of all Muslims throughout the world irrespective of citizenship or ethnicity. Muslims must be loyal to the *umma* above any other community, in theory.

Yathrib: the historical name for the oasis village in Arabia to which the Muhammad migrated in 622 CE, commonly knows as the City of the Prophet by Muslims today, or simple *the city* (*Madina* or *Medina*).

Printed in the USA
CPSIA information can be obtained
at www.ICGtesting.com
LVHW061934150823
755329LV00003B/60